CONFESSIONS
of a
Lost Sheep

All we like sheep
    have gone astray;
we have turned every one
    to his own way;
and the Lord hath laid on him
    the iniquity of us all.

Isaiah 53:6

For the Son of man
    is come
        to seek and to save
            that which was lost.

Luke 19:10

How think ye?
if a man have a hundred sheep,
and one of them be gone astray,
doth he not leave the ninety and nine,
and goeth unto the mountains,
and seeketh that which is gone astray?
And if so be that he find it,
verily I say unto you,
he rejoiceth more of that sheep,
than of the ninety and nine
which went not astray.
Even so
it is not the will of your Father
which is in heaven,
that one of these little ones
should perish.

Matthew 18:12-14

CONFESSIONS
of a
Lost Sheep

by Peggy Jones

lifting up the Light of the world

Wilson NC 27893

Library of Congress Cataloging in Publication Data:
Jones, Peggy, 1920-
    Confessions of a lost sheep / Peggy Jones.
      p. cm.
    ISBN 0-915541-87-4 : $7.00
    1. Jones, Peggy, 1920-   . 2. Jones, David, 1920-
3. Christian biography--United States. I. Title.
BR1700.2.J66 1991
209'.2'2--dc20
[B]   91-20254
                                            CIP

Unless otherwise indicated, scriptures are quoted from the King James Version of the Holy Bible.

Incident "*Go to the spa*" first appeared in *StarLight* magazine,
      copyright 1990.

Cover photo by Grant Heilman studios
Cover design by Jan Troske

Copyright 1991 by Peggy Jones and by
Star Books, inc.

Published by: Star Books, inc.
                408 Pearson Street
                Wilson, NC 27893

Telephone: (919) 237-1591

ISBN: 0-915541-87-4

First printing

CONTENTS

Dedicated to
the Lord Jesus Christ
who created this story
by His Spirit

Foreword

For many years, I have felt there just had to be a written account of God's faithfulness to my parents and their response to it. In God's perfect timing, that has happened. Certainly it is a great honor to be asked to write this Foreword. These are thoughts of a daughter, once rebellious and unappreciative, but through God's grace able now to see the treasure He gave her in her parents.

My childhood became rich with a Christian heritage that was drenched in prayer, as my parents took hold of the Scriptures and let the Scriptures take hold of them. That is the best legacy parents and grandparents can pass on to children and grandchildren. It has been my privilege and great blessing to watch these two from a special vantage point. Who watches you more closely than your own children? As we yielded to His way, God gave us harmony in our home. To put it simply, we loved living together.

Perhaps the key to seeing their three children happy in the Lord today was my parents' determination to hold fast and hold forth the Word of God--no matter what the cost. Their lives have been governed by God's principles, and they have resisted every temptation to compromise those principles. In their thirty-plus years of following the Great Shepherd, it has been their consistent practice to give God His part right off the top and to ask at every turn, "Lord, what would You have us do?" The results of such godly giving and living are told within these pages.

I am no prophet, but I believe someday my parents will stand, hand in hand, before the Great Shepherd. Able to look Him fully in His eyes, they'll hear the words we all long to hear Him say to us: "Well done, good and faithful servants." Standing with them will be the many they brought into the Kingdom through their obedience to Christ's command, "Feed my sheep" (John 21:16,17). As a pebble thrown into the water creates a ripple effect, these fed sheep will have brought in and nourished other sheep. And so it goes, as God's Word, sown and rooted in people's lives, is allowed to bear fruit.

It became David's and Peggy's calling to bind up the hurting and wounded, rescue the endangered, feed the hungry, and love them all. It will be our joy if this account of their experiences increases your desire to follow the Great Shepherd and heed His command: "Feed my sheep."

Gwen Jones Hanger
Moline, IL

Each and every one of us has one obligation, during the bewildered days of our pilgrimage here: the saving of his own soul, and secondarily and incidentally thereby affecting for good such other souls as come under our influence.

Kathleen Norris
American author, 1880-1960

Introduction

If we had known we were lost, my husband and I would never have stepped on that Pan American plane to Nicaragua.

"Well, then, why were you going on the mission field?" folks invariably ask when we tell them our story.

"Mainly to get Brownie points with the Lord," we answer. "Perhaps partly out of guilt. We were building a dear little cottage on the ocean when we heard of the need for a missionary couple in Bluefields, Nicaragua. It didn't seem right for us to enjoy our beach cottage and our delightful congregation in Riverside, New Jersey, if the Lord wanted us elsewhere."

We really had a heart for the poor--and besides, I loved business. Bluefields was in a part of Nicaragua that had been depressed ever since a blight had taken the banana crop some years earlier. Perhaps we could encourage someone in the area to develop a profitable enterprise.

But as for saving the lost--that was the furthest thing from our minds. We felt *everyone* was en route to heaven. Our job was to encourage people along the way.

Had someone asked me point-blank, "Are you a Christian?" I would have tried to stifle my contempt and said something like, "Why, I've always loved the Lord. I can't remember when I wasn't a Christian."

It's true I had always loved the Lord. When I was a very small child, sitting beside my mother at the Good Friday service, tears ran down my cheeks when the account of our Lord's crucifixion was read from the Bible. I had tithed from the first dime I earned, and had read the Bible and prayed each night ever since I heard a Christian should do these things.

I was born the first time on June 12, 1920. Like Nicodemus, I had no idea I needed to be born again. But God did, and He set about teaching me, giving me many adventures along the way.

> *Jesus answered and said unto him, Verily, verily, I say unto thee, Except a man be born again, he cannot see the kingdom of God.* (John 3:3)

> *But to all who received him, he gave the right to become children of God. All they needed to do was to trust him to save them.*
>
> (John 1:12 The Living Bible)

Peggy Jones

"Lord, what am I to do?" I asked, kicking aside some early fallen leaves as I walked home after a fruitless job interview. It was almost noon on a late-August day in 1938. I had graduated from high school in the spring and was eager to get on with life. But the Depression made college impossible and jobs difficult to find.

In May, the Animal Trap Company, the largest industry in my hometown of Lititz, Pennsylvania, had given a little hope:

"Come back later in the summer; maybe we'll have something then." Now--after three months at Lancaster Business School--my hope for employment was dashed: "Sorry. We're still laying off employees and can't take on any new personnel."

"Lord, I want to serve You. I need more schooling, but I can't pay for it unless I find work. What am I to do?" I asked again.

Suddenly, for no apparent reason, I stopped. My eyes had been riveted on the uneven pavement, partially covered with leaves. Looking up, I discovered I was standing at the entrance of Linden Hall Academy and Junior College. Linden Hall was affiliated with our church, but I had never thought of going there, knowing it was financially impossible.

"Go in and ask for a scholarship in Home Economics," a very distinct Voice spoke to my spirit. I was aware the Home Ec department had just been modernized and enlarged, but I had no way of knowing they were in need of students with that major.

Obedient to God's command--for I knew the voice was His--I turned immediately, walked to the door, and rang the bell.

Mrs. Corbett, the secretary, appeared. "Yes, Peggy, what can I do for you?" she asked.

"I'd like to see Dr. Stengel."

Although he was occupied with desk work, the headmaster agreed to see me.

Wasting none of his time, I remained standing while I introduced myself and made my request: "I'm Peggy Snyder, and I wondered if I might have a scholarship in Home Economics."

As I said it, I realized the idea hadn't been in my mind over two minutes.

"Why, yes," Dr. Stengel answered, with only a slight hesitation. "I think it can be arranged. Just go down to the dean's office, and he will give you the necessary forms."

I walked home on clouds, not on leaves. I was thrilled I could have two years of college as a day student, but even more thrilled that--for the first time in my life--I had heard the Lord speak to me! Perhaps if I learned to listen more carefully, He would speak to me again.

Life at home during those two years offered little opportunity for quiet meditation. While attending Linden Hall, I earned a little money by baby-sitting several evenings a week and by writing two regular columns for the *Lancaster Sunday News.* One was on girls' sports throughout the county. The other was a shoppers' guide, entitled "Shopping with Sue." It took several hours weekly to round up the material for these two columns, and then to write them.

Richard, my older brother, worked as a reporter for the *Lancaster New Era.* Every afternoon after work, he made a seventy-five-mile train trip to Temple University in Philadelphia, where he studied law. He returned to Lititz about midnight. Richard maintained this grueling pace for four years.

Bob, my younger brother, reversed the order. In the mornings, he rode with other students to Lancaster, where he studied at Franklin and Marshall College. After hitchhiking home for a late lunch, he worked as desk clerk at the local General Sutter Hotel from 3 to 11 P.M.

Our father, a banker, would gladly have sent us to college had he been able. Since he wasn't, we had to learn resourcefulness and management. Dad's bank had gone under during the Depression, and his new job as an insurance agent barely provided for the necessities. When he wasn't trying to make a living, Dad enjoyed hunting, fishing, politics, and volunteer service to the town and the church.

Mother was a phenomenal manager, and ran our home with the utmost efficiency. Take spring and fall house-cleaning, for example. The evening before the big effort, we children helped empty rooms, removing books from the bookcases and pictures from the wall. I loved returning home from school the next day to see and smell each newly cleaned room.

Our house was on a double lot, and Mother and Dad cultivated vegetables on one half; fruit trees, grapevines, and raspberries on the other. Mother canned over 400 quarts of produce a year, made her laundry soap from grease, and dried corn and apples. She even saved and dried out all cantaloupe seeds to feed the birds in the winter. In our home, thrift and management were caught as well as taught--good preparation for the Lord's service.

Mother wasn't just a homebody, however. She also taught a Sunday-school class and belonged to the board of our church's home for the aged, serving as president of that board for fifteen years. She was involved in the Red Cross during World War I and in welfare distribution during the Depression years. Active in the Delphian Society, the Sewing Club, and Farm Women, she also served as leader of a King's Daughters Circle and was the first woman to be elected an elder in our congregation.

In addition to her volunteer work, Mother served as a correspondent for the three Lancaster newspapers and for our local paper as well. She was responsible for reporting every newsworthy event in our town of 5000: fires, deaths, weddings, engagements, news from the public school and Linden Hall, meetings, reunions, and "personals." The newspaper wanted lots of names, and she would sometimes have several hundred for one reunion alone. When Richard came home at midnight, he sometimes found her typing away by her hunt-and-peck system. Some nights, he insisted on taking over and finishing so she could get some rest.

All that hard work must have been good for Mother. She's still living at 105.

After my first year at Linden Hall, I was allowed to change my major to Liberal Arts, while still retaining my scholarship. I also took typing and shorthand, in order to prepare myself for a job.

When I finished my two-year course at Linden Hall, I was able to get work as a secretary at the Morgan Paper Company in Lititz. My starting salary was $12 a week, which was divided as follows: $1.20 to the church, 12 cents for Social Security, $10 in a savings account for college, and 68 cents for spending money. Baby-sitting and a Saturday-evening job as assistant social editor for the *Sunday News* supplemented my income and provided for the necessities.

Soon after I began working, I applied for admission to Antioch College, which had a work-study program. Two students held one job--one working while the other studied--in alternate ten-week periods. I hoped to be admitted in the fall of 1941.

Although I dated sporadically during the years I was living at home, I was never seriously interested in anyone. As I left my teen years behind, I began to wonder about choosing a marriage partner. My preference would be a minister in our denomination, but I didn't know any likely candidates. I took my concern to the Lord.

"If You could lead Abraham's servant to find a wife for Isaac [see Genesis 24:1-27], I believe You can help me. And since You let Gideon use a fleece to obtain guidance [see Judges 6:36-40], perhaps You will honor that method for me. This is my fleece: If any man asks me to marry him, I will in turn ask him if he is willing to read the Bible and pray with me daily, and to tithe our income. If he says yes to both questions, I will know he is the one You have chosen for me."

On July 30, 1941--some time after my talk with the Lord--a telegram from Antioch College brought a drastic change in my life. "Need you in secretarial position here in office," it said. "Start August 5 and study B Division. Signed, Miriam Dickinson, Office Manager."

My cherished dream was about to be realized. Antioch College, located in the little village of Yellow Springs, Ohio, had 750 students. Two thirds were men-- an ideal situation for a female transfer student.

In the years after I went to Antioch College in August of 1941, many changes took place at home. The boys left home soon after I did, both of them going into the armed forces and serving in Europe during World War II. After the war, Bob settled in Bethlehem, Pennsylvania, where he became a vice-president of our denominational college and seminary. In emergency situations, he filled in as president of a local bank and served as administrator of St. Luke's Hospital. His last contribution, before his death in 1989, was to head the United Way Fund for the city of Bethlehem in 1986.

Richard, the lawyer, served in the Pennsylvania State Senate for twenty-two years, where he acquired the nickname "Mr. Integrity." Now semiretired, he writes two columns weekly for the *Lancaster New Era.*

Dad returned to the banking field during the war, and was sixty-six when he died in 1951. After being a widow for fifteen years, Mother married a lifelong friend, Harry P. Musser of Charleston, West Virginia, at the age of eighty. They had more than twenty happy years together. Their travels took them to Hawaii, South Africa, and England, where they met the Queen Mother. When Mr. Musser died in 1986, Mother, 100, returned to Lititz.

But all that was still in the future when I left for Antioch College, where I hoped to continue my spiritual quest while I prepared myself to do God's work.

How real was God, and could one know Him intimately? Would He speak to me again? I had to find the answers.

2--"He's the one"

The train I took to Yellow Springs, Ohio, left from the Lancaster station on Sunday evening, and I was filled with excitement as I told my family goodbye. I even liked the all-night ride on "The Jeffersonian." Outside Altoona, the conductor alerted us to watch the train make the famous Horseshoe Bend. Just as daylight broke, he called out, "Xenia! Xenia!" That was my stop.

The bus took a much disheveled me into the sleeping community of Yellow Springs, and to Morgan Co-op

Dorm, where I was to live with nineteen other girls. Sixty students ate in the dorm's dining room.

From the very first day, I loved the informal, friendly student body and faculty. Since my first ten weeks were spent in office work, evenings and weekends were free. In a glorious whirlwind of activity, I found campus life exhilarating as I became acquainted with stimulating students who had held jobs all over the United States.

Registration day in mid-October brought a change of faces and made me a full-time student. Most of the work-study students, having completed a five-week period of study, had returned to their jobs. Only those who, like me, worked on campus were left behind. At lunch that day, I found myself at a table with nine total strangers. The chap across from me said something humorous, and as I laughed I thought, *He would never be boring to live with.* An odd observation of a perfect stranger. After the meal, we both decided we wanted a cup of tea--even though I never drank tea. We talked until all the others had gone, and I was almost late for my job in the registration line. Among other pertinent facts, I learned that the fellow with the ready wit was from Youngstown, Ohio, and his name was David Jones.

That evening, I received a call on the dorm phone.

"Hi! This is your friend from lunch. How about going to the second show?"

What to do? I had a date with a town boy the next night for the same movie. Further, there was a dorm meeting that evening, and for that reason I had refused a date with another of the co-op fellows. *Suppose he never asks me again,* I thought. Perhaps I could suggest walking the shady back streets and thus avoid the possibility of seeing either of the other men. I made a quick decision.

"Yes, I can be ready," I answered.

The movie was *Citizen Kane*, with Orson Welles. Outstanding as it was, it proved to be a minor part of the evening. After the show, we sipped milkshakes in the nearby college hangout and discovered amazing similarities in our backgrounds and beliefs. For one thing, we were among the small minority of students who attended church. David always sang in the choir, whether he was at home, on campus, or off on a job. I got out my purse and showed him the picture of my home church that I always carried with me.

It was as though each of us, after five years of casual dating, had suddenly struck the jackpot. After the soda shop closed, we continued talking as we walked through the streets of Yellow Springs. It was ten minutes of two when we said good night in front of my dorm.

As I was crossing the threshold of my room, the Lord spoke to me for the second time in my life. "*He's the one,*" He said clearly.

The next evening, I sat through *Citizen Kane* with the town boy and thought I had handled it perfectly. But at the end of my next date with David, the subject of the movie came up. "By the way," he asked significantly, "how *did* you enjoy *Citizen Kane*?"

It seems the town fellow was a friend of David's, and had visited the library where David worked. They began discussing movies and discovered each of them had dated a new transfer student and taken her to see *Citizen Kane*. Imagine their surprise to learn they had dated the same person!

My full load of classes, part-time work, and active social life left little time for spiritual growth. When we were given an assignment in Social Studies to write our life's philosophy, I had a chance to evaluate. I realized

Peggy Jones

that, even though I had heard God's voice again, my faith hadn't grown an inch.

"I don't know a way to prove there is a God," I wrote. "But my prayers have been answered, and I feel His presence." There was more in that vein.

When the professor returned the papers, mine was missing. He asked me to see him after class.

"May I keep your paper to share in other classes?" he asked. Then he added wistfully, "Don't let anybody take away what you've found." Later, I learned he was a former Roman Catholic priest.

As the weeks flew by, David and I were together every possible minute. Once a week, we did the dishes together at the co-op. That meant washing and drying dishes and tableware for sixty people--without an automatic dishwasher. From early morning till late evening, we were separated only for classes or jobs. Then suddenly our happy little bubble burst.

On a lovely mild Sunday in December, we had been to church and were enjoying a leisurely dinner at the co-op. One of the fellows came flying through the door and yelled, "Grab your plates, everyone, and come to the basement to hear the radio. We're at war!"

We were a sobered group as we congregated on couches, chairs, steps, and floor to listen to the news bulletins about the Japanese attack on Pearl Harbor. Although we didn't know it at the time, some of our group would be wounded, some killed; others would be conscientious objectors, for Antioch College had a Quaker affiliation. All of us would be affected.

Later that afternoon, David and I took a long walk and talked about our future together. David was a year and a half away from his degree. If he was allowed to finish, should we marry first?

It didn't take long for us to make that decision--after I had obtained David's promise that we would have daily devotions together and would tithe our income.

Our wedding took place on September 20, 1942, in my home church in Lititz. Just as the minister pronounced us man and wife, the sun burst through the clouds and shone directly on the two of us. A sign of God's blessing? I believe it was.

David enlisted in the Army Reserves, and was allowed to finish work on his B.A. degree. I found a job in the office of the Eastern Pioneer Hybrid Corn Company in Yellow Springs, and we had seven months together before he entered the Army and I returned to my parents' home in Lititz. When I applied for a job at the Animal Trap Company this time, they were *delighted* to hire me as a wartime traffic controller.

3--"It's a girl!"

After orientation and tests at Camp Perry, Ohio, David was assigned to the Signal Corps and sent to Camp Edison in Sea Girt, New Jersey.

In a few weeks, he called to say, "I've found a room. It isn't much of one, but at least we can be together." As soon as I could leave my job at the Animal Trap Company, I joined him.

What a room it was! Bugs crawled on the wall. Thirteen people used one bath. Whenever a train went by, the whole house shook. Each military couple was allowed a small portion of a refrigerator shelf. Onions were rotting in the pantry. I was four-months pregnant and remember that odor to this day. But we *were* together, and we gave thanks for that every day.

We sought out a doctor, an elderly, genteel man in Point Pleasant. When he learned our address, he frowned.

"Get her out of there," he said to David.

"I'd like to, but there is no other place," he answered.

"Get her out of there!" the doctor repeated sternly.

David's Army duty and the job I had taken at a department store each required six full days a week. The only time we had to house-hunt was Sunday afternoon. We walked all over Manasquan (the town adjoining Sea Girt), but there were no rooms to be found. About dusk, exhausted and discouraged, we found ourselves standing before a substantial home displaying a permanent ROOMS sign. We had met with so many refusals it seemed useless even to ask.

Just then, the front door opened and a woman came out. As she was walking past us, David said politely, "Excuse me--but are you the lady of the house?"

"Yes," she answered, hesitating briefly.

"Is there any chance you have a room?"

"Oh my, no! My rooms are always taken. As a matter of fact, I have had my Army people move out, since I go on vacation tomorrow. I don't like strangers in the house while I'm gone."

We said we could understand, but did she know of anyone who might have a room?

"No, I don't," she answered thoughtfully. There was a pause; then she asked, "Aren't you the couple I saw in church this morning?"

"Well, we were in the Presbyterian church," we said.

"I was the choir member who had the violin solo. . . . Tell you what. Why don't you come in and see the front bedroom? If you like it, you can move in as soon as it suits."

Returning with us into her lovely home, she showed us a well-appointed bedroom with a private, white-tiled bath! Thinking of our college debt and the coming baby, I asked fearfully, "What is the rent?"

"Six dollars a week."

I could hardly believe my ears! We were paying eight dollars a week for our present quarters.

Seeing my look of amazement, she added, "I have another rate for officers."

We were overwhelmed by our landlady's kindness and God's goodness, and a few days later we joyfully moved into our beautiful new quarters.

Unfortunately, we didn't have long to enjoy them. After a few weeks, the boys of the 990th Signal Port Service were told one Saturday they would be shipped elsewhere in the States on Monday. Several of us service wives had jobs at Steinbeck's Department Store in Asbury Park, and we had promised when hired that we would give a week's notice before leaving. When the men came home Saturday evening and brought us the word they were leaving on Monday, the other wives made plans to go home immediately.

"Wait!" I said. "We promised Steinbeck's a week's notice. We can't just leave."

"Don't be silly," said Edna, who hailed from Brooklyn. "Who wants to hang around here with our husbands gone?"

On Monday, I was the only one who reported to work at Steinbeck's and gave my week's notice. When I returned to our room that evening, David came home too. Their unit's departure had been delayed. The same thing happened every day that week.

Returning from my last day of work on Saturday, I stepped into the Sea Girt train station to buy my ticket to Pennsylvania. The small room was jammed full. Even though I knew better, I couldn't resist asking the station-master, "Has the 990th shipped out?"

"I can't say, ma'am," he answered, handing me my ticket. As I turned to leave, a very tall GI, standing up against the back wall where nobody else could see, nodded his head affirmatively. Grateful to him for letting me know David was no longer there, I took the first train back to Lancaster and home.

After several months in Chicago, David's unit returned to Sea Girt. It was there he got the word, "It's a girl!" We had already picked her name: Barbara. She was named for my mother, who was herself a fourth-generation Barbara.

When Barbara was six weeks old, David hitchhiked to Lititz for the weekend. He arrived late Saturday evening with bad news.

"I can't say anything, but we must have the baby baptized in the morning." That meant, of course, they were shipping out to go overseas. David spent the next twenty-one months in Europe, while I lived at home.

Barbara, their first grandchild, was a great source of joy to my parents, and Mother was happy to care for her in the evenings while I took over Bob's old job as desk clerk in the General Sutter Hotel. I wrote David daily and lived on his letters. During this time, my spiritual growth was nonexistent. I prayed just one prayer over and over: "Please let the war end, and bring our men home safely."

One episode of this period involved a weekend visit to Washington, DC, with Richard's wife, Toylee. She was assigned to Walter Reed Hospital with the American Red Cross. That Saturday, she was scheduled to accompany a group of veterans to the home of Evelyn Walsh McLean, and she secured an invitation for me.

Mrs. McLean's spacious home, Friendship, occupied a city block, as I recall.

Our dinner was of nonrationed foods. (During the war, we were legally restricted from buying more than limited amounts of coffee, sugar, meat, etc.) After dinner, we adjourned to a large room. Mrs. McLean chatted with us, then brought out the famous Hope diamond and passed it around so all the guests could handle it and wear it if they chose. After a group picture was taken, we dispersed to various parts of the room.

Those veterans who were able, and who had wives or dates with them, danced to the music of a band. Others played games. I chose to sit in on the conversation of a group which included Mrs. McLean, a Supreme Court justice, and a prominent socialite.

Riding home on the bus, I reviewed the evening. Somehow it came through that neither fame nor fortune brought happiness. I felt utterly satisfied with my goal of following spiritual pursuits.

In May of 1945, the war in Europe ended. We waited impatiently for David's turn to leave. Finally it seemed he would ship out by mid-December. I quit my job at the hotel, and for seventeen days barely left the phone.

Christmas came, and there was still no word from David. Instead of giving Barbara her gifts, I kept them on hold until her father could enjoy watching her open them.

Years later, I learned what David's holiday had been like. When the hostess at a seasonal party asked the guests to tell about their favorite Christmas, David had no hesitation.

"It was 1945," he said. "I was on the high seas coming home from the war on the *Mahanoy City*, a troop ship. I was in the bow of the vessel, getting the worst of the waves. A hurricane hit us, and we rose and fell helplessly. I was terribly seasick--but even so, deliriously happy. I was going *home!*"

The long-awaited call finally came on New Year's Eve, 1945, about seven o'clock.

"I have a collect call from David Jones," the operator said. "Will you accept the charges?"

"Will I?" I screamed. "You'd better believe it!"

After almost two years, I finally heard my husband's voice.

Before leaving for combat, military personnel weren't permitted to tell anything. Now David couldn't have been more specific.

"We'll be discharged at three o'clock Sunday afternoon, January 6, at New Cumberland, Pennsylvania. Can you meet me?"

I met him.

4--"What am I doing with these cards?"

David and Barbara and I lived in my parents' home until we could get our bearings. With so many GIs returning, jobs were hard to find.

While David was a student at Antioch, he had held a co-op job at Howe Military School in Howe, Indiana. Now a contact with Colonel Bouton, the headmaster, led to a teaching position in the middle school. We moved to Howe in late summer, and settled into a second-floor apartment in the home of a retired college professor.

Howe was a charming little village with only 500 residents and three churches: Episcopal, Presbyterian, and Methodist. David was required to attend Episcopal services at the school, but I took Barbara to the Presbyterian Sunday school.

The grocery store where we shopped was owned by a Methodist--a kind, likable man. When his church held a revival, he brought the visiting preacher to call on us. I remember the horror I felt as I saw them approach the house. Surely this man would want to pray--and he might get loud about it! Our landlady was a high Episcopalian, and I felt sure she would disapprove of any such goings-on in her home.

To this day, I can't remember how the matter turned out. I only know we remained lost. Had our pride not been an inch thick, we might have saved ourselves another ten years of wandering in the desert.

Barbara was two and a half when we moved to Howe--and like all the wives with young children, I stayed home. Since we took our lunch and dinner in the mess hall, my household duties were not strenuous. Bridge was our pastime. A lovely life if you enjoyed children and bridge, and I did.

One day Barbara and I were walking to town, where we usually went to the library before doing any shopping. As we entered the square, we saw everything was closed.

"Oh, dear!" I exclaimed. "It's Washington's birthday."

Barbara had just celebrated her third birthday, and she thought such occasions were nothing to be sighing about. Then she figured it out.

"Oh, my!" she said. "And we never sent him a card."

Although David and I continued our daily devotions and tithing, any spiritual progress was imperceptible. Since we were paying off his college debt, we lived very carefully. We had no car, but we could walk to town for groceries, and friends were kind about inviting me along on shopping trips elsewhere. Our refrigerator was an old-fashioned icebox. David would walk to the ice plant and carry a huge chunk of ice home on his shoulder.

Our only luxury was our tithe money. By giving 10 percent of each paycheck to the Lord's work, we felt rich when it came to giving. One experiment in giving was especially rewarding. It came about as a result of reading the Sunday *New York Times*, which our landlady thoughtfully put on our steps after she was through with it. A full-page ad for CARE packages to be sent to Europe stated that ten dollars would buy forty-six pounds of food, to be delivered to an addressee specified by the donor.

"Wouldn't it be fun to send one to somebody?" I asked David, who was also behind the pages of the *Times*.

"Yes--but who would we send it to?" he wondered.

I didn't have an answer until I remembered reading in our church paper about a group of 200 Christians who had fled on foot from East Germany, taking only what they could carry with them. Impoverished, they were living in old army barracks in West Germany under Spartan conditions. "Why not try them?" I asked.

David gave his approval, and I sent a check to CARE in early fall. The address given in the written account was quite vague, so we held little hope the package would reach them. We directed that, if undeliverable, it be given to others.

Months went by, and we heard nothing. As I thought about it, I realized 46 pounds of food for 200 people was almost a joke.

Then one spring day a letter arrived from Germany. It reported that on December 23 the group received notice a parcel was being held for them in Alexisdorf, the nearest town. The next day, one of the men made the long trip on his bicycle to collect the package. By the time he returned with the parcel, the group had gathered for their customary Christmas Eve vigils. (In order to hold their traditional services with brass-band accompaniment, they had brought their trombones in wheel-barrows with them to their new home.) They opened our gift--the first contact they had had with America since the war--and gave thanks for this sign of love from church people across the ocean.

Their profuse gratitude and the description of their hardships made us want to do more. We were given the name of a family about our age, whom we were able to help for a time.

One day as I was sitting at the bridge table, the Holy Spirit reminded me of the commitment I had made to the Lord back in Lititz. I sent up a silent prayer: "Lord, I told You years ago I wanted to serve You with my life. What am I doing here with these cards?" There was no answer, and the bridge games went on.

In our second year at Howe, Gwen was born. As the school year drew to a close, David broached the subject of our future.

"Where would you like to settle, Peggy? I feel it's time to make a change, and I'd like this to be our last move. I think we should be in the East, because our folks might need us."

My mind went back to the summer of '39, when Kay Miller and I had visited another Linden Hall friend, Ella Tuthill, who lived in Southold, on the north fork of Long Island, New York. I remembered a delightful day at Southampton, lying on the beach. "If I ever have a chance to choose where I want to live, it will be eastern Long Island," I had commented to Ella.

Remembering that remark, I suggested to David that he send a resume to the school in Southold. Mr. Williams, the principal of the school, offered him another middle-school post, and David accepted. My friend Ella (now Mrs. Bill Mosher) found us a lovely old house in Southold, on Town Harbor Lane. At the end of the summer--which we spent with my parents in Lititz while David worked on his Master's degree at the University of Pennsylvania--we moved to Long Island on Labor Day, 1948.

Meanwhile, David and I were still searching for more reality in our Christian walk, and after finishing summer school he attended a three-day silent retreat near Wallingford, Pennsylvania. Although I knew it had affected him profoundly, I was totally unprepared for the surprise he gave me one evening in November, as I was serving dessert.

"The Lord has told me I am to go into the ministry," he announced out of the blue. "I will finish out my contract with the school for this year. Then we must move to Bethlehem for me to attend seminary."

Since my dream had been marriage to a minister in our beloved denomination, this was thrilling news for me. However, we were both twenty-eight, and we had two children. Barbara was four, and Gwen just turning one. And when David applied at the seminary, he was told he could not work for at least two years, since he would have to take extra courses in Greek and Hebrew along with the regular seminary courses.

Rather than letting the financial problem dissuade us, we began to pray for the Lord to show us how to handle it. Before we were married, we had agreed that, if we were blessed with children, their welfare would come first; therefore we felt I should stay home. With that in mind, we wondered how the Lord could possibly supply our needs.

The north fork of Long Island had two major sources of revenue: summer tourists and potatoes. Neither could be of any profit to a housewife looking for income in the winter. Daily I asked the Lord to show me what I could do to help financially.

While we were at my parents' home during Christmas, my brother Bob showed us a line of informal notepaper bearing sketches of scenes in our hometown of Lititz. Realizing Long Island had nothing similar, I began planning a line of notepaper showing scenes from the north fork. A friend, Libby Ward, made the sketches for me.

I received 1200 boxes of notepaper on April 1 and sold them all within three weeks. Feeling we had a winner, I asked Dad to send all our war bonds so we could order more sets. By fall, when we moved to Bethlehem, we had five assortments covering all of Long Island. After settling in Pennsylvania, we had notepaper made up showing scenes from Staten Island, Princeton, Philadelphia, the Poconos, and Lancaster. We also had many individual orders for churches.

For four years, everything I touched seemed to turn to money. All our needs were met, and we were able to give generously to church causes. We never had to have sitters, as one of us was always able to stay with the girls. We felt this miraculous provision for our needs showed the Lord's approval of our desire for me to be at home.

Besides being profitable, my business venture proved to be an educational experience. Alice Roosevelt Longworth invited us to tea at Sagamore Hill, and I met Dr. Einstein in his home--the subject of one of our sketches in Princeton. He gave me an autographed copy of his recently published book, *Out of My Later Years*.

In all this, I was just as lost as ever--but didn't know it.

5--"Is there really a heaven?"

During our year in Southold, David had the eighth-grade homeroom. One of his star pupils, Dick, was a neighbor. The boy's mother and I had become friends and frequently had tea together.

One June day near the end of the school year, a neighbor brought us dreadful news: "Dick's been killed!" It seems Dick's father had employed a man to clean up the lawn, and Dick was helping him. As they were hauling refuse to the dump, a train hit their truck at an intersection covered with foliage. We were stunned by the tragedy.

At the funeral, David was a pallbearer, and I chaperoned the class. Somehow, we got through the service-- but when we went to visit Dick's parents after it was over, I realized my theology was poor. I had no comfort to give them.

"Is there really a heaven?" I asked David as we were dressing to make the call. He didn't know any more than I did. We hoped so.

As it turned out, Dick's mother and father needed to talk out their grief, and the question of heaven never came up. But I faced the issue privately. "Lord, *is* there a heaven? I must know." Dozens of times a day I brought the matter to Him.

In late August, shortly before we moved to Bethlehem, I drove off with my notepaper for an overnight business trip. East Setauket, about thirty-five miles away, was my first stop.

The lovely village green was peaceful and deserted. I made my way through the historic Episcopal church to speak to the minister's wife about having the church women handle the sale of our notes. Nobody was at the rectory or at the church.

I lingered in the ancient cemetery. Looking at the headstones, I mused: *All these folks were alive a hundred years ago. Now they are gone. Where? I must know. Is there a heaven?*

With that, the sky opened up, and I saw light such as I've never seen before or since: beautiful, bright light, not glaring or painful to the eyes. Music was the only other element--ethereal, heavenly music. The vision was so brief I had no time to distinguish anything more specific. I longed to be drawn up into the light, which seemed so restful and peaceful, in contrast to my over-busy life. When the heavenly light faded away, I returned to earth amid the tombstones.

Although disappointed that I hadn't been privileged to go to the source of that light, I consoled myself by thinking, *No, we have work to do. David must go to seminary and then on to ministry. The girls must be raised. It's not time yet.*

In a daze, I returned to the car. My next call was to be at the Stony Brook Gift Shop nearby. But the very thought of talking dollars and cents was repugnant. I turned around and drove home. The family was surprised to see me.

"I was just thinking, I'd rather you did this," was my weak explanation to David. Not yet ready to discuss my private revelation, I stayed home and pondered it while he was gone.

In a few days, I realized I was not asking the Lord any more if there was a heaven. He had not answered my question in theological terms, but He had given me proof. I was grateful.

Our move to Bethlehem, Pennsylvania, came at a time of housing shortage. Veterans were getting settled, and housing hadn't caught up from war years. Through the hospitality of my brother Bob and his wife, Helen, we had a place to stay during the weeks it took us to find suitable housing--a third-floor apartment.

David settled in happily to studying again, and I thoroughly enjoyed seeing old friends from earlier years and making new ones. We seminary wives had a group called Seminari-annes, which met monthly. The group was small and friendly and felt like family.

After completing the first two years of seminary--the usual load plus Greek and Hebrew--David was given a student charge in Hellertown, Pennsylvania, during his third and final year. We moved, note business and all, into the parsonage. In a short time, we were stagnating spiritually as we tried desperately to keep our heads above water.

For David, the burden of a new work, in addition to his studies, was stressful. I spent a good forty hours each week on the note business, which was still necessary to supplement our income. The girls, now seven and three, needed more time than we could give them. The church women felt--or else I did--that I should match whatever church work they were doing. As I tried desperately to measure up on all fronts, I found myself exhausted all the time.

When David had to be gone one weekend, an ordained minister was obtained to preach and baptize babies. That weekend, both the sacristan and the sexton were also out of town, so I had to handle all the preparations for baptisms and a guest pastor. The girls and I cleaned the church on Saturday, and I had the minister to dinner on Sunday. About all I recall of that meal is that I burned a big pot of green beans.

As David phased out of his training period, I sold out the note business. A bookstore owner whom I respected found a buyer for me and suggested a price. I felt it was too high, so I promised myself I would check with the buyer in two years and, if he felt I had overcharged him, would refund part of his payment.

When the two years came to an end, we were financially strapped, and I was sorely tempted not to write the buyer. Prodded by my conscience, however, I did write, and the buyer replied that he was satisfied. What a relief!

6—"From now on, you work for Me"

In 1953, after David had completed the three-year seminary course, we were ready for a call.

Our first full-time church was in Riverside, New Jersey, where the congregation was known to be one of the most friendly, agreeable, and cooperative in the denomination. To say we were happy during our two-and-a-half years there is to make an understatement.

Having sold out the notepaper business, I was going to support David 100 percent in his ministry and try to be a better mother. A few months after our move, however, we took one of David's Mondays to visit Long Beach Island, a two-hour drive from Riverside. We were so charmed with this section of the Atlantic coast we began to think of buying a piece of land and building a cottage there. I scoured the gift shops and found there was no line of notepaper depicting local scenes.

"David," I said enthusiastically, "these shops have no local notes. And Long Beach Island is made-to-order for a set. It will be the most profitable one yet, with all the influx of summer trade. In fact, it'll be such a piece of cake I think I'll have coasters made up too. We can get a TV and clothes and dear knows what all else with the profits."

I was about to learn a hard lesson. Those notes and coasters simply would not sell. If a shop actually took them, they would be tucked in some out-of-the-way corner and would never need replenishing.

As the third tourist season rolled around, I determined to try the gift shops one more time. The first one I visited was in Surf City. Both the owners were there, and I proudly showed them the notes and coasters. After all, I had had seventy-nine active accounts on Long Island when I sold out my first business, and nobody had ever been indifferent or refused to take the notes.

One owner looked at the other. "Who would want them?" she asked. The partner didn't know, so I packed up my samples and left.

Walking to the car, I spoke to the Lord. "Lord, what is the story?"

For years, I had met with success everywhere I had gone with the notes. In Philadelphia, Wanamaker's handled them exclusively. In Princeton, the University bookstore sold hundreds each year. *What*, I wondered, *could possibly account for such a change?*

Then the Lord spoke to me for the third time, very clearly so I would never forget. *"You asked Me to get you through seminary, and I did. From now on, you work for Me."*

So that was it. All my previous success had come from Him. Now His help was withdrawn. Furthermore, He was making it clear that, no matter how much I might be tempted to work outside the home, I was not to do it. In years to come, there were many times when I felt I should contribute to the family income. But I always remembered this clear directive that we were to trust Him and put all our efforts into the ministry.

Before that word came to me from God, we had already purchased a piece of land at 505 North Atlantic Avenue in Beach Haven. It was on the ocean, in the heart of town--an ideal location.

We drew up plans for a simple beach cottage, only 24 feet square. Contractors put in the plumbing and poured the concrete base. David spent his free Mondays and vacation time in our garage, nailing together eight-by-eight-foot sections of the walls. After several months, the twelve sections were finally ready to be taken to the site.

A young man in our church volunteered his truck and offered to drive David and the sections to our lot. But he had heart problems, so he couldn't help unload. As they took off about dark on a Friday evening, I was concerned. I admonished my husband to find a good place to sleep and hire ample help in the morning. He was his usual positive, trusting self. It would all work out, he assured me as he kissed me goodbye.

"You mean," I said kiddingly, "when you arrive, five or six angels will be waiting and say, 'Is this what you want unloaded?'"

"Something like that," he said cheerfully.

After beseeching prayer, I went to bed and fell asleep.

About one o'clock, I was awakened by the sound of David's key in the door. I couldn't believe he was home so soon. "Whatever happened?" I asked, amazed.

"You'll have trouble believing this, but it was exactly like you said. Russ McHenry saw us load up, so he recruited a carload of men from the church, and they got to the beach ahead of us. When we arrived at our lot to park the truck for the night, there they were, all ready to unload. It's all finished!"

Knowing the Riverside men, I could believe it. How we thanked the Lord! In short order, thanks to Willis Bucher and his crew from Lititz, the cottage was erected and under roof. We were never to enjoy a vacation there, however. Our whole lives were about to change.

7--"Show us what's missing"

Our congregation was launching an evangelistic program that had us all drawn into service. The plan was for David to list all the prospects for our church in the area. Then, while a week of services were conducted by a pastor from another province, members of the congregation would call on those families and invite them to attend the next night's meeting.

I had an uneasy feeling all day Monday, for that night I was to go calling on the unchurched. Normally I was super-eager for any and every church activity, but this one gave me an uncomfortable feeling of inadequacy.

As I joined the others in the basement of Hahle Hall before the service that evening, I discovered I wasn't the only one feeling inadequate. Everyone seemed uncertain. One question seemed to be on all lips: "What do I say? What do I say?" The visiting clergyman gave a pep talk and had a prayer with us, and then we headed for the door. Althea, my partner, declared loudly, "Well, I'm lucky. I have the minister's wife with me, and *she* knows what to say!"

As I grasped the handrail to go up the outside steps in the dark, I said silently, "Lord, You and I both know I don't know what to say either."

Althea and I chatted as we walked down to Bem Street, where we were to call on a man living alone. Meanwhile, I was begging the Lord to have him not be at home. As we approached his house, I saw his lights were on, and I changed my prayer to "Lord, please let him have company." But he didn't.

Our "prospect" invited us in and offered us seats. We talked about the weather, then about his canary. Having nothing further to say, we got up and rather lamely invited him to come and visit our church. He was noncommittal, and we left without pressing the point.

That evening pinpointed thoughts I'd been having about church, and I couldn't wait for activities to end. The visiting pastor finished his coffee at our kitchen table about midnight. As soon as he left and David bolted the door behind him, I blurted out what was on my mind.

"David Jones, I don't know about you. But I know that, for myself, there has to be more to the Christian religion than I have found. What difference is there between a church member and someone who doesn't attend church? Our members like each other's company; we enjoy the hymns and love the Lord, but basically there is no real difference between us and the world. If heaven is for real, where is the dividing line between those who make it and those who don't? What are the criteria?"

Poor David! He was tired. It had been a long day, and he only wanted to get to bed. But I was too worked up to be brushed aside easily. So he did what he usually does in such cases. He said, "Let's pray about it." Together we knelt at the couch.

"Lord," he prayed, "if there is something we've been missing, please show us." And with that, we called it a day.

The campaign was a huge success. We took in many new members--fifty-five in one service. That was so special the Secretary of Christian Education and Evangelism came from church headquarters for the unusual event.

Between the beach cottage, the congregation, our girls, and outside activities, we didn't have time to reflect much on our prayer. David, thanks to a judge in our congregation, served on several state boards and was a charter member of Rotary. Besides all my church duties, I was active in PTA and the Woman's Club. In addition, our house had somehow become a sort of center for ministerial friends to drop in and chat over coffee. The Presbyterian pastor in nearby Delanco would enter our kitchen door, fill the teakettle with water, put it on the stove, then call us to come. Life was full and fun, and we thoroughly enjoyed it. But the answer to David's prayer was on the way, and it involved a decided change in our lives.

It started on a Sunday afternoon, with a phone call and an invitation. Gerry Eichman, whose husband was the pastor of our sister congregation in nearby Palmyra, said happily, "Can't you come over for the evening? A couple from Bluefields, Nicaragua, are visiting us, and I think you'd enjoy meeting them."

David and I talked it over, called a sitter, and went, never once remembering that the bimonthly meeting of our local ministerial couples' group was scheduled for that night.

The missionary couple from Nicaragua, the Dregers, told us about their work in Bluefields, located on the east coast of Nicaragua. They stressed the need for another couple there--a need that was obviously very much on their hearts.

David and I had never, for one minute, felt a call to the mission field--but we had dedicated ourselves to be wherever the Lord needed us. As days and weeks went by, the thought of the need for a couple in Bluefields disturbed us more and more. Finally, we decided to go to the Mission Board and see if it was a call. We were actually hoping the head of the Board would relieve our minds by saying he didn't consider it a call. Then we could continue on our happy course.

"I believe this is a call from the Lord," Bishop Hamilton said. "We've been praying for a couple there, and since it's an English-speaking congregation, you won't need to be fluent in Spanish."

Talk about a change! We could only imagine how different our life-style was going to be and how many complications our move would entail.

Mother, recently widowed, was heavy-hearted. She and I, her only daughter, had always been close. David and I had to examine Scripture. "Children, obey your parents" (Ephesians 6:1) was clear. But in the next verse, adults are told only to "honour thy father and mother." We felt it was not dishonoring Mother to obey God's call to the mission field, and that the Lord would look after her. He did.

The cottage was nearing completion. Our friend Pete Pfau said he would look after that.

We would learn Spanish as a courtesy to the country. The Board felt it best for us to spend six months in Managua for language training before going to Bluefields. My brother Richard and his wife, Toylee, offered to keep Gwen, seven, and Mother was delighted to keep Barbara, eleven, so the girls could go to school while we studied. That arrangement proved to be a godsend, though the separation from our children was hard.

There was one thing I knew I couldn't handle. Before we announced our pending move, I asked the Lord to please give us help in packing. Being a pack rat by nature, and somewhat poorly organized besides, I knew I would need help. The Lord answered my prayer through one of His dear handmaidens, Mary Bueno. She offered to devote two evenings a week and all day on Saturdays to helping us pack. What a blessing!

One day I learned of a project being undertaken by the Woman's Clubs of the nation to restore Independence Hall in Philadelphia. I immediately got in touch with Mother, since she had two of the original Windsor chairs from the Hall, which her great-grandfather, Conrad Hertzler, had purchased at an auction around 1800. They had apparently been much used and often painted, but when they came into Mother's possession they were carefully cherished. She had them refinished, and they graced our fireplace for years.

The family agreed unanimously that those chairs belonged back in Independence Hall. The committee in charge of the restoration project couldn't wait to get them, as they had never expected to locate any of the originals. Though we had no proof of the chairs' origin, it all fit together, as the chairs that were originally in the Hall were known to have been sold in small lots at about the date Conrad Hertzler made his purchase.

When Mother agreed to sell the chairs to the committee, she asked permission to have her grandchildren's pictures taken in them. Our final errand, before we left the country, was to make a trip to Philadelphia so Barbara and Gwen could have their pictures taken sitting on their grandmother's chairs in Independence Hall. It was an elegant goodbye to life as we had known it.

8--Culture Shock

We spent the night with Cousin John Fusco in Miami before leaving for Nicaragua in September of 1955. A hurricane was moving in on Central America that day, and we were sure our flight would be canceled. Amazingly, it left on schedule.

After a brief stop in Cuba, we ran into torrential rains. The plane circled Managua for two hours before a break in the clouds finally made it possible for us to land. It was a close call, as the gas tank was almost empty.

The Pixley family drove through the flooded streets to meet us at the airport, and they were our hosts for several weeks until we found suitable living quarters. Dr. Pixley was a Baptist missionary doctor, and his wife a nurse. They were in charge of a lovely hospital there, newly built by the Northern Baptists.

We finally found lodging and board with a bilingual family, hoping to pick up the language more quickly than if we lived with English-speaking people. We found our own teachers--a native young man who taught English at the Cultural Center and a woman missionary, Barbara Kuper.

The Union Church, a nondenominational congregation formed for English-speaking Protestants, provided spiritual fellowship as well as pleasant social activities. Its hundred members included Embassy employees, military personnel, workers in the U.S. Foreign Aid Program, and business people from the United States and Europe. Some of the east-coast Nicaraguans from our denomination also belonged, since they spoke English. There was talk of beginning a church for the east-coast folks, but so far none had been started.

There was distinct cultural shock as we visited the market, where meats hung out in the open, covered with flies. Bread was, of course, uncovered, and huge hunks of a whitish cheese were displayed on the floor, along the aisles. The smells under the low ceilings, in tropical heat, defy description. Babies slept in boxes under the counters.

Within six weeks, I was suffering with amebic dysentery and was barely able to make it to our Spanish classes. The home where we lived was in the heart of the city, and rats and roaches ran rampant. Sanitary facilities were poor, and flies swarmed over the entire neighborhood, indoors as well as outdoors. Oranges served at breakfast always tasted of onion, so we knew the cutting board wasn't cleaned from day to day. The evening meal usually consisted solely of fried foods. My poor stomach!

Except for problems of sanitation, health, and homesickness for the girls, things were fine. Our host family was friendly and likable. Joanna Cope from Oregon, a teacher in the American School, also boarded there. Her refreshing sense of humor was a continual joy as all three of us adjusted to the culture. A typical exchange went like this:

Joanna, on arriving home from the heart of town: "Well, it happened."

We: "What happened?"

Joanna: "What I always knew would happen."

We: "What?"

Joanna: "I got spit on."

Eventually, thanks to a couple with the Foreign Aid Program--Everett and Mona Cree, from Iowa--a home in the country was found for us, and my health improved.

As we completed our six months of language training, we were eager to go to our assignment. Although we knew David was to serve in Bluefields as assistant pastor of Central Church, the largest congregation of our denomination in the country, we still had no inkling of the Lord's real purpose in bringing us to Nicaragua.

A horse-drawn wagon jostled and jolted our belongings laboriously up the hill to our new home. Miraculously, none of the bone china was even cracked or chipped. All had arrived by ship at the local dock, called El Bluff.

We were assigned to the mission house, built next door to the mission chapel. Our comfortable home consisted of two bedrooms, a combination dining and living room, kitchen, bath, and two small rooms on either side of the hall in the front of the house. We also had an outhouse, necessary in case of water shortage. Water from the roof was collected in barrels for kitchen and bathroom needs.

"Look at this!" I exclaimed excitedly, as I saw the ideal arrangement for home-schooling. "This can be your study," I told David while standing in the left front room, "and the room across the hall will be the girls'."

In that room, under my tutelage, Barbara would go through the eighth grade and Gwen through the third. Simultaneously, they would take Spanish in order to attend our mission's school where, by government law, all teaching had to be in that language.

The chapel next door would serve for midweek services, Sunday school, and youth-group meetings. I was the leader for our local young people, while David had a group down at Central Church. Turn-out was no problem, as twenty to thirty young people would usually come to the meetings in the chapel. "Sword drills" (competition to see who could find Scripture references first) and singing made for spiritually edifying evenings in general.

When our denomination celebrated its five-hundredth anniversary in 1957, I wrote a play for the young people to present. Church was the center of their lives and ours too, and we were happy together.

Housekeeping presented some problems. The first morning, I simply could not get a fire going in the range. It's a long wait for a cup of coffee when you try to start a fire with green wood. We ended up purchasing a two-burner kerosene stove for rush needs.

Another adjustment was mosquito nets. One day I walked into the bedroom, where David had laid a pair of trousers on the bed. I counted forty-seven mosquitoes congregated on the trousers, holding a convention. We had to sleep under netting at night, and we could almost count on it: when we had tucked in all the edges and felt safe, a mosquito had always managed to be inside.

Peggy Jones

We had our own method of gauging the humidity. As we walked up the hill following the Sunday-morning service, the sweat dripped from David's chin under normal conditions. If it dropped from his nose, the humidity was high. But when we saw droplets running from his ears, we knew the saturation point had been reached.

As soon as we were settled and the school year was over, Barbara and Gwen flew down to join us. Dr. and Mrs. Thaeler (denominational missionaries stationed in Nicaragua) were returning from the States and kindly took our daughters under their wing. I flew to Managua to meet the plane. The girls loved our set-up, and we were all happy to be together again. Without stateside distractions, family life was even more enjoyable.

In many ways, life in Bluefields was idyllic, in spite of the heat and humidity and mosquitoes. Not many folks are privileged to turn the clock back sixty years, as we did in Bluefields. Since there were no roads to anywhere, only a few cars were seen on the streets of the town. You could get in and out of Bluefields only by boat or plane. The slow-paced life gave an old-world charm. Although there were a few telephones, I don't recall ever using one.

Seven gardenia bushes--called jasmine by the local folks--grew four to five feet high in our yard. The fragrance from a huge bouquet of the blossoms on our dining-room table was almost overwhelming.

A tall breadfruit tree in our front yard yielded a large, starchy fruit shaped like a good-sized cantaloupe. When boiled, it was mealy and utterly unappetizing. After we learned to slice it and fry the slices in deep fat, we found it better than potato chips. Mangoes, papayas, bananas, and limes were a delight in their seasons. Fortunately, rice and beans were always available.

Shrimp came in about twice a year. Midmorning would bring the welcome cry: *"Shocaline, shocaline!"* As a young boy passed the house bearing his basket, I would grab a pan and a *cordoba* (worth fifteen cents in U.S. money) and buy a pint of shrimp--heads, tails, and all.

Our neighbor to the rear, Mrs. Halsall, knew how North Americans missed their vegetables. One day she lovingly showed me a climbing type of spinach she had planted by our mutual fence so we could help ourselves. Is it any wonder we loved our people so much?

Every so often, I would try to gather enough of an assortment of vegetables to make a kettleful of the vegetable soup we all enjoyed. On rare occasions, a boat would stop by the bluff where ships unloaded, and Mercantile, our leading store, would have carrots and beets to sell. At Christmas time, they even had apples and celery--a real treat.

One day, we had as a luncheon guest a Harvard man who was gathering research data in Bluefields. Lacking other vegetables to add to the carrots, rice, and dried beans in my soup, I was driven to stripping a bush of tiny peppers. Assuming they were merely a Nicaraguan facsimile of our northern pepper, I meticulously cut, seeded, and diced them.

After the blessing, I brushed my hand against my cheek. It burned. Not believing it, I brushed my other cheek. It burned, too. Then we started to eat the soup. Now I knew the real meaning of *hot* peppers! The soup was hot enough to take your head off. Even the cat refused it. What we ate in its stead, I have no idea.

Central Church was downtown, overlooking the lagoon. While listening to the Sunday-morning sermon, we could gaze through the open windows on the peaceful blue water, sometimes dotted with a fishing boat or two.

Occasionally this pleasant reverie was interrupted by our dog Boots, a small, "Heinz 57" variety. He was the most spiritual and best-educated dog in town. If we failed to tie him up, or if he got loose, he would trot the half-mile to divine service, hasten down the aisle to our pew, and curl up at our feet, his tail thumping loudly on the wooden floor. If we didn't get him immediately, our senior pastor would pause and say, "Whoever owns that dog, please take him out." Whereupon David would grab Boots' collar and, as he resisted every step of the way, drag him out of the church and take him home. When school was in session, Boots would locate and visit Barbara's or Gwen's classroom.

Besides Boots, we had a cat, a parrot, and a chicken. We named the chicken "Sunday Dinner," but she produced and raised eight chicks before living up to her name.

Nicaragua is famous for a cutting ant. In one evening, these tiny creatures, the size and shape of the common ant in the United States, stripped every green leaf from one of our large gardenia bushes. They hauled them off in small pieces and kept up an endless, well-organized march till the job was done. Poison to kill these ants was sold, oddly enough, at the bank.

Many of the folks in our congregation were Jamaican and were very refined. I cringe to remember my sleeveless dresses compared to their more modest attire. The older ladies never appeared at a church service in anything but long-sleeved dresses. Slacks and shorts for women were unheard of. Schoolgirls had shorts for gym class, but when girls in the neighborhood came to play in our yard with Barbara and Gwen, they wore skirts over their gym shorts to walk to our house.

No stores carried ready-to-wear dresses. One bought material, looked in magazines for a style, then took the material and picture to a dressmaker. She would take measurements and produce the desired dress, which would fit perfectly.

The whole area was economically depressed. When David went calling each afternoon, he often found such stark poverty he felt compelled to share the money in his wallet, even though our small salary was already stretched to the limit. We didn't know how to deal with this dilemma, and prayed about it. One afternoon, after dressing to make his calls, David was about to walk out of the bedroom. Suddenly, a thoughtful look came over his face. Pausing, he reached into his hip pocket, pulled out his wallet, and threw it on the bed. Then he walked out. That was the only solution. We simply couldn't supply the needs of the whole community.

Our area of town, known as Old Bank, had electricity only a few hours each evening, and I had to wait till then to use the washing machine. With each gyration of the Maytag, our lights would brighten and then dim. Thinking the fluctuation was caused by a drain on our current, I instructed the family to gather around our dining-room table to read, and to turn off all the other lights.

One day a neighbor casually mentioned I had done the wash the evening before.

"How did you know?" I asked.

"Oh, we always know when you wash. All our lights flicker till you finish."

From then on, I washed very late in the evening, when I supposed the neighbors would be in bed.

One rainy day I complained at the dinner table about the problems of getting the wash dry. After all, we had 210.8 inches of rain that year!

"You don't use your head," David proclaimed. "Since you have to keep the cookstove going anyway, why not rig up a dryer of sorts?"

"Sounds great," I said. "Suppose you do it."

Using green wood, he made a frame to fit into the oven. After the heat from cooking a meal had subsided somewhat, we loaded the rack with underwear--the hardest thing to dry--and put it in the oven. Half an hour later, we eagerly opened the door. Lo and behold, we discovered big brown scorched spots on all the undergarments. Here and there, holes had burned through the fabric. That was the last time David mentioned a dryer.

In July, one of the months with heaviest rain, there were thirteen funerals in our church. The cemetery was a sea of mud, and David had only one black and one white Palm Beach suit. After each of the thirteen burials, inches of splattered mud had to be gotten off the trousers. I ran out of women willing to tackle the job of washing them, at any price.

Another experiment that fizzled was my homemade root beer. We had brought some bottles of extract from the States--but, alas, no recipe. I took a guess at it, and the result was pretty bad. One day our senior pastor, Mr. Shimer, and one of the elders, Miss Tody, stopped by to rest on our porch after taking communion to a sick member in our area. They were quite proper in their white outfits.

Wanting to offer them a cool drink, I said, "All I have is water and root beer that didn't get quite right. Which do you want?"

Naturally, they voted for the root beer. After their first sip, Brother Shimer looked at Miss Tody and said, "I won't tell if you don't!"

I tried one more batch. David had an outstation trip up the river and needed to take boiled water. I figured root beer would be just as thirst-quenching and more of a treat. It sloshed and jostled all day in the hot tropical sun as the bottle lay in the open boat.

By evening, he had arrived at his destination and was to hold a little service for the family where he was staying. Before beginning the service, he poured himself a drink from the bottle I had provided. Immediately eight-year-old Maritza piped up, "Hey, I smell rum!"

That was my last attempt at making root beer.

One of the elderly women in our church had organized a little King's Daughters Circle for girls, and Barbara and Gwen were members. One week she invited me to attend. I was sitting there minding my own business, perhaps woolgathering a bit, when I heard her say, "And now we'll have Mistress Jones tell us all about the Holy Spirit." She sat down and looked at me, as did the whole class. I was completely taken aback, and have no idea what I said.

After the meeting was over, I lingered to talk with the leader, and the girls went on home. On arriving home, I got to work in the kitchen. David came in casually and, with mischief in his voice, said, "Do tell us *all* about the Holy Spirit!"

At that time, I didn't know enough even to be curious about Him.

9--Three Days on a Banana Barge

Soon after our arrival in Bluefields--before the girls had come to Nicaragua--a Christian Endeavor group from our congregation invited David and me to join them on a three-day boat trip up the Escondido River. This group of ninety people wanted to be a blessing to the folks in isolated areas who seldom if ever could attend services. The brass band would play, a seminary student would preach, and David was asked to serve communion, wearing his white surplice.

Though we moved as fast as the old banana barge allowed, it seemed a most leisurely pace. Off and on all day, we sang hymns to the accompaniment of the band. When the sun was too hot up on deck, we sought shade in the hold below. (Not long afterward, the bottom fell out of the rather antiquated barge. How did the Lord keep it afloat with ninety people in it?)

As time for the first meal arrived, I wondered what they could possibly provide. But somehow rice and beans were cooked, and there was even a special treat for David and me: a small plate of sliced tomatoes with mayonnaise. The dear folks knew how we from the States love salad. How does one receive such a loving gift? Though beset by poverty, these Christian brothers and sisters delighted in giving to others things they didn't have themselves. A humbling experience for us.

After a long day of travel, we finally reached the lone farmhouse where we were expected. In total darkness we glided along, delighted to see a solitary kerosene lantern being swung to guide us in to shore. We were singing, "Through many dangers, toils, and snares, I have already come; 'tis grace hath brought me safe thus far, and grace will lead me home." How reassuring to know that, though we were tucked deep into the interior of the country, removed from any phones, planes, cars, or roads, we were still safe in His care.

I had been wondering how so many people would sleep. The answer was quite simple. The men slept in the field and the women on the boat. Having brought a folding youth cot belonging to one of the girls, I set it up in the captain's quarters. Four women sat on a bench on either side, sleeping propped up against each other. One other spent the night on a stool. I alone had the luxury of a bed, albeit it was shorter than I. My head all but touched the front wall.

No sooner had I fallen asleep than the dear ladies felt obliged to waken me. "Mistress Jones! Mistress Jones! A rat ran along the ledge right by your head." I awoke, surveyed the situation, and told them, "Ladies, if he doesn't bother me, I'll not bother him." Then we all fell asleep.

During the next two days, the barge stopped at various landings along the river, and we held preaching services in private homes. The trip had been carefully planned, and folks throughout the area had been alerted as to the approximate time of our arrival--so there was always a good-sized gathering. On Sunday morning, we held communion in an abandoned church building. For the Christians who came, it must have seemed like a dream, to join with almost a hundred of us singing the familiar hymns to the accompaniment of the brass band, and to have a minister, wearing the traditional white robe, serve them the elements. We felt good about the trip.

When the Sunday service was over, the barge headed downstream as fast as possible. Since there would be no moon, it was important for us to be in familiar waters by dark.

About three o'clock, the boat made an unexpected stop at Rama--the only town we passed.

"We'll be here forty-five minutes," the leader announced. "You may visit the town, but be sure to return on time."

As David and I stood there, trying to decide which way to go, Brother Eddie, a leading elder in the church, spoke to us.

"Our denomination bought a lot to build a church when they thought a canal might come through here. Would you care to see it? It's across town, but if we walk fast we can make it nicely."

We agreed, and the three of us hastily made our way through the pathetic town. Churches were boarded shut; saloons were wide open. Raucous music hurt our ears, and we had to detour around drunkards lying along the street.

"There!" Brother Eddie pointed to a lot of un-mowed grass. "That's it." Then he thoughtfully looked at the house next to the lot. "I know those folks. Mind if we step over and say hello?"

When he knocked on the door, a timid woman opened it very cautiously. "Eddie!" she screamed, hugging him. She invited us in, and told us a sad tale.

"We are the only Christians left in town," she said. "We can't afford to move. The town is so wicked and sinful, it is hardly safe to leave the house."

David looked at his watch. "May I read the Bible and pray?" he asked, assuming he could. As he finished, we rose to leave.

With tears streaming down her face, the woman said to us, "This morning I felt so alone and forsaken. I went into the bedroom and got down on my knees. 'Lord,' I prayed, 'if You still know we are here and care about us, please send me a sign *today*!'"

We hugged her goodbye and rushed back to the barge, which took off immediately. No explanation was given for this one departure from the schedule. Nor was any needed.

One day, some of the young men in the congregation approached David. All of them fervently desired to become ministers, but none of them had much education. In order to qualify for the denomination's *Instituto Biblico* (seminary) up at Bilwaskarma, one had to have a high-school diploma. These men were in their twenties and thirties, with wives and children to support. They had to work during the day, but they wondered if David would hold a training class for them one night a week.

Thinking of all he had to offer them, David agreed. After all, he had a B.A. degree from Antioch College and a B.D. from the seminary.

Still being of a liberal mind, David felt the class should deal with a wide variety of issues. One night monthly they discussed current events, using our *Time* magazine. Another night each month was devoted to spiritual and biblical questions. When David gave answers offhandedly, they invariably asked, "But what does the Bible say?"

Still another evening, they worked on economic improvement. That was where I entered in, since I loved business. We latched on to brooms. It seemed our little town imported all its brooms from Managua. All it would take to make our own was to raise broom straw and gather the handles out in the bush. The only cash outlay would be for nails and cord to fasten the straw to the handles.

Our friends with the agricultural department of the U.S. Foreign Aid Program in Managua gladly sent us fifty pounds of seed to plant for the straw. We sent part of the seed to a young farmer in Pearl Lagoon, twenty kilometers up the river. His first planting got rained out; the second was eaten by rats. Our local men also tried raising broom straw and had similar disappointments. I was beginning to understand the frustration these dear folks felt after innumerable unsuccessful attempts to help their economy. We never made a single broom.

The fourth and most important evening meeting each month was given to preaching. As the men gave practice sermons in the chapel next to our home, David sat in the back taking notes on grammatical errors, sentence structure, style, etc. Before beginning his sermon, each man would give his testimony--a practice that was new to us. One man's testimony had a life-changing impact on David.

"I was working in a sawmill seven days a week," the man said. "Each Sunday morning I would hear the singing from the church across the way. One Sunday I looked down at my clothes. 'O Lord,' I begged, 'if only I could get some shoes and a new pair of trousers, then I could go to church and get saved.'

"With that, the Lord spoke to me: *You don't need shoes or clothing. Just kneel down here on the ground and give your heart to Me.*"

He did just that, and his face shone with the light of heaven as he told about it.

David was both touched and disturbed. When the class ended, he went into the bedroom, got down on his knees, and prayed, "Lord, please do for me what You did for him."

David arose a new man in Christ and said the feeling reminded him of what he had experienced on June 24, 1944, during the war. His unit had just landed on Omaha Beach, Normandy, France. The men were ordered to dig foxholes or find some other shelter for the night. In the dark, he was happy to see the outline of a Royal Canadian Air Force vehicle.

With a great sense of security, he settled under it. As expected, Bed Check Charley, a lone German bomber, came overhead and bombed the harbor, but not his immediate area.

Early the next morning David crawled out from under the truck and was horrified to discover that its front fenders carried two red flags--indicating a cargo of high explosives.

What he thought was safety was just the opposite. How like the person depending on his denomination, his good deeds, or anything else other than trusting in Jesus to get him to heaven. Only Jesus saves.

Soon after we left Bluefields, the brother whose testimony brought David to Jesus was given a pastorate. That was thirty-three years ago. Now he is pastor of one church and, we hear, overseer of several others.

Three other men in that class also became pastors, and two of them were in active ministry until their death. One, a beautiful brother in Christ, had two sons drafted into the Sandinista army; he may have died from heartache and worry. Another man eventually became pastor of the large Central Church in Bluefields. We've lost track of the other members of the class, but it's quite likely some of them served small congregations. None of these men were urged to become ministers. They all just loved Jesus so much they wanted to win others to Him.

One of the highlights of our stay in Bluefields was a conference for young people, held at Pearl Lagoon. David was the director. A few weeks before the conference began, he received a letter telling him one of the teachers he had recruited couldn't attend.

"You're going to have to teach the class on conversion," David said as he swung around toward me in his swivel chair after reading that letter.

"*Me!*" I exclaimed. "You know I can't figure out if I've had a conversion experience myself. Why would you choose me?"

"You're the only one with the period free," he answered.

We prayed about it, and David suggested I invite both national (Nicaraguan) and United States leaders to share their testimonies at each session. This proved to be an inspired suggestion.

Each day, we listened raptly. To me, the best testimony was that of a middle-aged national pastor known and loved by all.

"When I was a young man," he began, "I lived a wild and wicked life. Despite my praying mother, I cared nothing for my soul. Then one day I was out in the lagoon in my dory, alone. A storm came up and blew my dory over in deep water. I couldn't swim. The boat cap-sized, floated away, and I went down. I cried out to the Lord, begging Him to save me. If He would, I told Him, I would live for Him the rest of my life.

"Just as I surfaced, a huge log came floating by. I managed to grab it, and eventually got to shore.

"From that day on, my life has been different. The Lord forgave all my filthy sins, and made me a new crea-ture in Christ."

For twenty years, this pastor had been a living proof of the transforming power of Jesus. His testimony, and that of the other leaders, gave me much to ponder on the boat trip home. There had never been a time in my life when I asked Jesus to come in and make me wholly His. I had never confessed my sins--pride and com-placency, for starters--nor had I ever asked God for cleansing with the blood of Jesus, forgiveness, and salva-tion. I began to have a continual gnawing within.

The conference had been a success. To the great relief of our girls, no lizard or monkey had been served. (One of the missionaries had tried to prepare them for the worst by telling what had occasionally been served in former years.) We did have turtle, one big enough to feed a hundred people.

Even today, as those youngsters of the fifties are spread throughout Central America and the States, I'm sure they remember nostalgically the beauty of finding a spot in the quiet of Pearl Lagoon early in the morning to be alone with the Lord.

One morning, after school had started and David had left to hold the chapel service down at the *Colegio* (the mission school), I was alone in the house. I knelt by our living-room couch. Though I knew nothing of altar calls, I felt that becoming a Christian should lead to a momentous change in one's life. And I knew there had never been such a change in mine. I had received teaching in the church, especially through the biblical liturgies; but somehow it was just head knowledge. Now I needed a heart experience.

"Lord, please help me. I want to be a real Christian. Just going to church and following the denominational rules hasn't changed my life."

I knelt there for an hour or so, reasoning, pleading, weeping, and confessing my sins before the Lord. I'm sure I invited Him into my heart and life, though I may not have expressed it so clearly. The important part was the attitude of my heart. I truly had "a broken and a contrite heart," which God will "not despise" (Psalms 51:17).

Gradually I began to feel peace, as I realized I had received cleansing and forgiveness. I finally rose to my feet and tried to sort out my feelings. Knowing so little about the second-birth experience, I had to grope my way along. I sat on the couch until David returned--and when he did, I found I was not yet able or ready to share my experience. Yet I knew that the Peggy who rose to her feet was not the same one who had knelt before the Lord earlier that morning. Finally, I was a "new creature" (see 2 Corinthians 5:17).

10--Two Second Chances

Tooth troubles were nothing new to me. By the end of 1956, I knew I needed to get to a dentist over in Managua. I made a plane reservation for Wednesday, January 23, and a dental appointment for the following day.

Several nights before my scheduled departure, we had a surprise visitor. Rarely did anyone come calling late in the evening, especially in a heavy tropical downpour. When we opened the door, we were amazed to see our elderly senior pastor, Mr. Shimer.

As always, he came directly to the point. "Brother," he said, looking at David, "I've just realized I can't go to Managua Thursday, to hold the service for our folks there. I must be in my office Friday morning for those who miss Preparatory Service. You will have to go instead."

(Custom had it that, in order to take communion, a member had to attend a preparatory service, at which time he was to examine himself and ask the Lord's forgiveness for any sins he had committed. Should he miss this service and not receive his ticket for communion, he must go to the pastor's study on Friday morning. The taking of communion was a very serious matter, as indeed it should be.)

My heart sank. All my plans would have to be canceled.

"That won't be necessary," David said to him. "I can go down to your office on Friday." He knew how much Brother Shimer enjoyed the change of pace, and he also knew of my plans to be gone Wednesday and Thursday.

We waited as Mr. Shimer thought it over. I was tempted to tell him about my own need for David to be at home with the girls, but decided my teeth had a lower priority than the Lord's work.

"No," he finally said. "I think I had better stay."

With that, I couldn't resist complaining. "Oh, pshaw! I wanted to go to the dentist then."

Mr. Shimer gave his characteristic shrug of the shoulders and said he must be going.

"Now what?" I asked David when we were alone. "Everything is set." Then a pleasant thought occurred. "Say, wouldn't it be fun to be over there together? We'd have a good time seeing old friends. Maybe Klara would stay with the girls." Klara was one of the missionary teachers at our church's school, and we often visited together.

The next day, however, my hints to Klara produced no results. Reluctantly, I wrote the dentist and canceled my appointment.

Wednesday afternoon, January 23rd, as I was finishing up dinner preparations, David came home from calling. "They are very concerned downtown," he reported. "Today's plane never arrived in Managua. They are sure it crashed."

Not until we were eating dinner did I remember I was scheduled to be on that plane. After dinner, I paid a visit to the Shimers.

"Thank you for saving my life, Brother Shimer. Nothing but your change of plans would have prevented my going on that plane today," I told him.

He had a thoughtful look as he realized how the Lord had sovereignly intervened. That trip up to our house was the only one he ever made just to deliver a message.

In a day or two, the plane was found. It had crashed into a volcano in the middle of Lake Managua, and all sixteen persons aboard were killed. Of the six from Bluefields, three were members of our church. If I had been on that plane . . .

On the day the funerals were held, I was asked to substitute for a mission-school teacher whose relatives had been killed. As I walked to the school, I saw Brother Shimer leave his home in his black suit, Bible and hymnal in hand. He was heading for the church, where many were already assembled. I had the strangest feeling, knowing how easily it could have been my funeral too.

As I entered the school, I sent up a prayer of gratitude: "Thank you, Lord, for giving me another chance at life at the age of thirty-six. Help me to use it wisely."

In the tropics, it is necessary for missionary families to have a helper in the home. The weather is so hot, and labor-saving conveniences so nonexistent that it would have been impossible for me to have gotten everything done without one. Our full-time worker, Christina (not her real name), did a fine job of keeping the house clean, as well as helping in the kitchen and with laundry. One day, the organ was open when the dusting was done, and someone later closed it. "Well," David said smugly as he passed by, "look at this. I can write my name on the organ."

Barbara, thirteen, was sitting nearby reading. Without batting an eye or looking up, she quipped, "My! Isn't education wonderful?"

Christina was twenty-one years old, and an answer to prayer if ever I saw one. She had a sunny disposition and fitted herself into our family beautifully.

Her grandmother had raised her in the village of Pearl Lagoon. After she finished sixth grade, there was no way financially for her to come to Bluefields and attend the mission's high school. But the longer she was with us, the more I realized that she had the ability to benefit from further education.

"Christina, did you ever consider being a nurse?" I asked one day as she was mopping the living-room floor. I could visualize her coming into a hospital room with a cheery "Good morning" that would gladden any patient's day.

"Oh my, yes!" she answered as she stopped mopping and propped her chin on the mop handle. She looked out over the lagoon in the distance and smiled dreamily. "I would often imagine myself a nurse. But there was no way to go on in school." She had no bitterness or resentment. She was simply stating a fact.

"You know we'll be seeing Dr. Thaeler next week at the church conference," I told her. "I'll ask if there is any way you could take nurse's training."

Dr. Thaeler was founder and head of our mission hospital up near the Honduran border. Since I had an appointment to see him about a medical problem on the first day of the conference, I was able to speak with him then about Christina.

"All nursing students must have a high-school diploma," was his immediate response to my question. "We can't make any exceptions."

Since I had to be hospitalized for an operation, I had plenty of time to think about the situation. When the conference ended, David and the girls flew home while I stayed on to recuperate from surgery.

On my last night in the hospital, I was wakeful. I couldn't bear to think of disappointing Christina.

When Dr. Thaeler came for his final visit the next morning, I told him my dilemma. "There just has to be an answer," I said. "But what is it?" (In Nicaragua, there was no such thing as a nurse's aide program.)

"Well, why can't she go back to school" he asked, "and get her diploma?"

"At twenty-one! Start seventh grade?" The thought was new.

"That's the only solution I see," he said, dismissing the case.

Weak and wobbly, I took the noon plane to Bluefields. I had gotten a light case of malaria after surgery, and my weight had gone down to 101 pounds. As I made my way down the path to the airstrip in the heat of the day, hoping I wouldn't faint, I checked to see if any animals were on the landing field. On our arrival, the plane had had to swoop low twice to drive some horses off the airstrip. Fortunately, the coast was clear this time, and the plane was almost on time. It was a welcome sight.

Once aboard, I turned my mind again to Christina. "Lord," I prayed, "I need a sign from You. Do *You* want Christina to be a nurse? If You do, please let me have an opportunity to see Elizabeth Marx and to be alone with her so we can talk. As superintendent of the school, she can advise me. If she thinks it's a good idea, I'll approach Christina about starting school next week."

Now that was a long-shot fleece! Plans were already made to have the town taxi meet me at the airport and take me straight home to bed. I couldn't expect to see Elizabeth for some time.

As I got off the plane, David had the girls and the taxi in tow. At the first chance to talk, he had a proposition.

"There is a birthday, and the teachers are having a dinner at their home. They'd like us to come. They said you could go to bed there. Then, after the meal, we'll have the taxi come and take us home. Do you think you could do it?"

"I'll sure give it a try," I said weakly. These birthday dinners were bright spots socially, and I knew how much the girls would be hoping we could go.

That's how it happened that, within an hour, I was resting on Elizabeth's bed when she came into the room, and we were alone to talk! I wasted no time in telling her about Christina's situation.

"I see no reason why she couldn't attend the *Colegio*, if you can handle it and she's willing," was her assessment.

When Christina came back to our house on Sunday, I began by telling her how some of us up in the States earned our own way through college. I had figured out a schedule and presented the way I felt we could work it out if she wanted to try working her way through school. Bless her, she was eager and excited. She got material for the required school uniforms and had them made in short order.

In a few days, Christina and Barbara were both in seventh grade. In the evenings, they did the dishes together and talked about school. How grateful we were when the first report cards came and both of them had made the honor roll! Barbara had mastered Spanish to an amazing degree, as all books and teaching had to be in the national language.

When we moved to Managua, Christina went with us and transferred to the Baptist school there.

Folks told us it couldn't be done, but Christina's putting herself through school worked so well that when we were to leave on furlough, five different people asked her to work for them, school and all!

As it turned out, Christina decided to work for the missionaries following us. But as they had several small children and needed more help than I did, Christina felt led to leave her job. Meanwhile, my mother's Sunday-school class in Pennsylvania sent Christina monthly support till she finished her five years of schooling. Then she took her nurse's training at the Baptist Hospital in Managua. Following graduation, she was given a position as director of the nurses in training. Later she came to the States, to the DC area, where she's been nursing ever since.

Christina and I were glad that God gave each of us a second chance.

11--"Get a good lawyer"

We had been in Bluefields a year and a half when David came in one morning and tossed a radiogram in my lap. "Here," he said. "See what just arrived."

Opening it, I read, "The Board of Union Church requests you to become our pastor." It was signed by the chairman of the Board of the church we had attended in Managua. How nice that our dear friends wanted David to come!

We felt the Lord's purposes for us in Bluefields had been fulfilled. Bringing forth young nationals (residents of the country) to carry on the work is fundamental to every mission, and David realized his most valuable contribution in Bluefields had been his training class for men. The Holy Spirit had placed in the men's hearts the yearning to win people to Christ. It had been David's joy and privilege to be the vehicle God used to help them develop their God-given natural abilities.

With the approval of our mission, David replied to the board in Managua that he was interested only if he could divide his time between Union Church and the establishment of a separate mission church for the east-coast Creole people. The board agreed to this proposal, and we began packing.

Before we left Bluefields, however, we threw ourselves into one final evangelical push. The Mission Board had arranged to send a man down from the States for a week of services. He preached dynamic messages, stressing the need for a new life in Christ.

What a week that was! Many people gave their hearts to the Lord. By the end of the week, some saloons were closing before dark, as they had no business. In our area of town alone, David married thirteen couples in one day. They had been living together but had lacked the means and motivation to marry. Now, having committed their lives to Christ, they wanted to get things right. We prayed for them to find a way to buy the license and get the clothes customarily worn for such a sacred ceremony. David received a gift that covered the license fees, and item after item was prayed in for each couple. Many of them had grandchildren to witness their weddings.

As we flew out of the Bluefields airport to cross the mountains, we had a glorious feeling of mission accomplished. Best of all, we ourselves had found Jesus, whom to know is life eternal.

What a sense of humor the Lord has! To answer our prayer, made back in the New Jersey parsonage, that He show us what was missing in our lives, He sent us to the mission field. There we learned, from the men David was teaching, that *Jesus* was the missing ingredient. It took more than two years in Nicaragua to accomplish our salvation--but our new life in Christ made every minute of those years worthwhile.

David hit the ground running when we landed in Managua. Now he *knew* what he was to do.

"One of our east-coast men [whom we'll call John] is in the hospital," a member of our congregation reported. "He tried to take his life by drinking battery acid."

When David got to John, he was ready and eager to pray the sinner's prayer and receive Jesus into his heart. He lived only a few weeks, but in a rasping voice he witnessed to others in his ward and led several to Christ.

His funeral was one of total victory. He didn't go empty-handed to meet the Lord. Although his life prior to his conversion had been totally without purpose, he left this earth in a blaze of glory.

David's two congregations made a pleasant combination. Union Church averaged 125 or so in their morning service, and our afternoon mission group somewhat under a hundred. The mission half of our responsibility had many facets. We ran errands and did purchasing for all eighteen or so missionaries in outlying stations. Our home served as a guest house for any church needs.

Then there were the congregational duties, which involved more than I thought they would.

"Alejandro, I wouldn't stay in that *pension* [boarding house]," David counseled one of our men from Bluefields who had come to Managua to work. The boarding house he had chosen was known to have late-night parties with much drinking. Alejandro took David's advice and found another place to live.

The next week, a young man on a bicycle came to our door and delivered a summons for David to appear in court. The owner of the *pension* was suing David for slander and defamation of character. We dropped everything and drove over to see our Baptist-missionary friend, Dr. Pixley.

When we told him what had happened, he looked serious. "You can't take this lightly," he said. "Get a good lawyer. Then pray. Pray for the Lord to turn it for good."

We did both. The case got front-page coverage, with pictures of David and the *pension* owner. The headline read (in Spanish, of course): CURIOUS CASE IN COURT YESTERDAY. The story reported the judge's profound amazement that anyone opposed drinking. "You mean you don't drink water either?" he had asked David.

According to the law, the plaintiff had to prove David had *publicly* said things against her. When she failed to produce two witnesses from our congregation to testify that David had spoken from the pulpit against her boarding house, the case was dropped. The Lord had answered our prayers that the trial become a testimony for righteousness.

Thanks to a gift of Spanish Bibles, David was occasionally able to minister to some *mestizos* (peasant farmers) who came into town to sell their produce. At dawn on market day, he would station himself in front of our home and hand a New Testament to each farmer coming to market. They all showed reverent appreciation. Along with their verbal "*Gracias*," the women would give David a curtsy.

Nacatamale suppers were a favorite form of gathering for our mission congregation. *Nacatamales* consist of cornmeal, pork, olives, and seasoning wrapped up in a large banana leaf and steamed all day. Socials were occasionally held in our home after work hours. The dinners would be ordered in advance and brought in piping hot.

Periodically, David and a leading layman from the mission church made bus trips to Puerto Somoza to hold a service for the stevedores. On other occasions, he went on two-day ministry trips to Puerto Corinto. One of our former helpers--we'll call her Mary--was working there. She wanted David to come and hold a service for our many folks whose work kept them far from church.

The first time I saw him off on the train to Puerto Corinto, I was so concerned, I sent bottled water and bread with him. I envisioned him sleeping on some dirt floor. When his return train was due, I was waiting at the station, dripping with anxiety.

"What a wonderful time!" was his first report.

"Tell me all about it," I said eagerly.

"Well, Mary works for Colonel Lamport, the officer in charge of port operations. He sent his chauffeur in a jeep to meet my train, and we had the service in their spacious home. Fans kept the air moving continuously. Afterward, the Lamports served *fresco* (a cool drink) and cake to all who came. When the folks left, the Lamports and I visited till late. We had such a good exchange!

"Yesterday I made my calls, but took meals with the Lamports. What feasts! Bacon from the States--ice cream, too. They get food from the ships."

By that time, my sympathy had turned to envy. Later it turned to gratitude, when those dear folks invited the whole family to come with David on his next trip. And we got to swim in the Pacific Ocean!

The girls attended the American School, which met from seven in the morning till noon and offered no extracurricular activities. One oppressive Sunday afternoon, sitting in service with Barbara, fourteen, on my right and Gwen, eleven, on my left, I had a talk with the Lord: "It's been so long since these girls have had any fun, they don't even know to miss it. I can't imagine how, but could You give them a little treat?"

Leaving the service, we saw a strange couple sitting in the back. When we stopped to speak to them, they told us they were with the United Fruit Company in Puerto Cabezas and were friends of the Befuses, our missionaries in that town. As we were chatting, a thoughtful look came over the lady's face.

"I'll tell you what!" she said suddenly. "Why don't you go home and get the girls' swimsuits, then meet us at the Gran Hotel? They can swim while we visit, and then we'll have dinner."

"Thank you, Lord!" I said as we drove off for a lovely evening.

Some things were downright funny, like the matter of our driver's licenses. City traffic was horrendous, and we hadn't driven in two years. Union Church supplied a car for its pastor, however, and it was mandatory David get a license.

"I'm not getting a license," I told David. "I'd never pass the test, even if I could understand the inspector's Spanish. I'll just stay in the backseat while you drive." Having failed two driver's tests in my youth before finally getting my license, I wasn't about to be humiliated in Spanish.

We started in an isolated area. David was instructed to make this turn and that until we were on Roosevelt Boulevard, the main street. Then he was told to park--in quite close quarters. After that, the officer turned around and motioned for me to come forward. Thinking it over, I decided it would be more difficult to explain than to move up front.

I pulled the car out and took off--and passed! Give credit to the Latins. They are a laid-back, relaxed people. From then on, I always had a soft spot in my heart for the Managua police.

One day an emergency arose for Ken, our missionary in the gold-mining town of Bonanza, and his family. His wife took their daughter to the States, where she was diagnosed as having osteomyelitis. Since this would require a long period of treatment, the Mission Board felt that Ken and the three boys should go home too. Ken wired David to handle the details involved in his leaving the country. David took care of all but one item of business, which Ken himself would do.

The scheduled time for the arrival of Ken's flight in Managua found us waiting at the airport. When the plane from Bonanza was late, the pilots of the States-bound plane agreed to wait as long as possible. But there would be no time for Ken to take care of the last pressing detail.

David called the U.S. Embassy. Charley, the person who could handle the matter, was not a member of Union Church. He was a hail-fellow-well-met type, lots of fun. We had a kidding relationship with him, but he owed us nothing. However, he agreed to accommodate us, on one condition: "That you buy me a beer, Davy. Ha, Ha, Ha!" With that, he hung up and immediately took care of Ken's situation.

Miraculously, Ken and the boys made it in time to get their flight to the States. Now to take care of our end of the bargain--getting Charley's beer. That evening we lurched along an unfamiliar street after dark, trying to locate a little store. We dared not let any of our dear mission folks find us buying beer.

When we got it, we plastered Scripture verses all over the bottle. The one over the cap read, "Consider your ways" (Haggai 1:5). We left the bottle at Charley's home.

We didn't see Charley for weeks. One day we entered the airport to hear raucous laughter at the far end. It was Charley, reliving the fun he had had out of his "favor."

Several evangelical missions joined forces with us in holding a young people's conference out in the country by a small lake. Each youth took a cot and slept out under the stars. It was dry season, so there was no concern about rain.

Our precious Christina did the cooking at the camp, and did it well. The director--Bob Porter, our Baptist missionary friend--provided a generator and a refrigerator. I stayed home and prepared some foods, which were picked up daily. For the last meal, I had seven or eight chickens made into chicken a la king.

The conference was a spiritual highlight, I'm sure. All the missionaries who took part were born again and zealous for souls. Almost all the young people made a profession of faith. They came home on a spiritual cloud.

We ourselves still had much to learn. One day Wilma Porter, Bob's wife, referred to Jesus' coming again, as though she really expected Him. I was amazed.

"How do you know about that?" I asked.

"Oh, it's all there in Revelation. I have a wonderful book about it. Would you enjoy doing a study on it?"

"Yes, indeed!" I answered emphatically. David was eager, too.

Each morning, after we dropped the girls off at the American School, we would go to the Porters' home at the Baptist School and learn of exciting prophecy. To think Jesus can return any day! And that He *will* come for us, because He promised. This awareness changed our whole outlook. The Bible worded it well when it referred to His coming as our "blessed hope" (Titus 2:13).

In 1959, our time in Nicaragua was drawing to a close, though we didn't know it. The girls and I planned to fly home in mid-July, as I was expecting our third child in September. David was to stay on six more weeks till our furlough was due.

Sometime in June, a boy appeared at our door with an invitation. The United States Ambassador was hosting a Fourth-of-July party, and we were invited.[1]

We were to begin festivities by gathering on the lawn for the flag-lowering. David and I stood in the back of the crowd. Just as the bugler started playing taps and the flag was being lowered, two limousines pulled up behind us. President and Mrs. Luis Somoza

----

1. We had paid a courtesy call on our ambassador soon after returning to Managua. His one topic was how much the Communists were infiltrating the country. It was obvious he found it alarming, while none of the rest of us were remotely aware of any activity. The year was 1958. It was to take twenty-one more years before the Communist takeover was completed.

emerged from one, his brother and his wife from the other. They stood at attention with the rest of us.

When the ceremony was over, we turned around to introduce ourselves. Imagine our surprise when the President said he had been told to get in touch with David regarding a matter in Pearl Lagoon. David took care of the matter through his church connections.

It was unfortunate President Somoza died prematurely within a few years. He had a real heart for the people. History might have been different had he lived.

After the girls and I left the country, David felt a very clear leading from the Lord that He was releasing us from the mission field. The verse given was: "Go home to thy friends, and tell them how great things the Lord hath done for thee" (Mark 5:19).

David and Christina packed up only those things we had to have. The rest he sold or gave away. Knowing David, I suspect all was given away.

Our four years in Nicaragua had yielded the ministers in Bluefields, and a good start for our mission in the capital. The huge bonus for us was our own conversion.

12--Skeleton in the Closet

"The next call I get, I feel we are to take," David announced one day in the spring of 1960. Since our return from Nicaragua the previous summer, he had refused several calls to churches, feeling none was the right one. We had enjoyed Mother's apartment in Lititz, and our newborn, Ann, was a blessing to all of us.

After returning to the States, David had gone to North Carolina for a brief course in Pastoral Counseling. Then he became the first chaplain, on a part-time basis, at the Lancaster General Hospital. The school year was now drawing to a close, and it was an appropriate time to make a change.

"Ephraim, Wisconsin," David announced when the letter came. "Ever heard of it?"

"No, can't say I have."

Before long, we heard all right. My brother Bob waxed eloquent about Ephraim, as did our friend Miss Myrtle Eckert, a music teacher. Ephraim was on the thumb of Wisconsin, in air-conditioned Door County. A resort community, it boasted an annual music festival under the leadership of the late Thor Johnson, a fine Christian gentleman.

What a delightful set-up! The large picture window in the parsonage overlooked Eagle Bay and Peninsula State Park to the south. Watching the winter sunsets on the ice was an experience of beholding God's glory such as we have seldom had. I was totally happy.

There was a one-room schoolhouse where twenty-three children, grades one through eight, felt like a family. Our Gwen and Bill Wedephol comprised the seventh grade. Barbara was a senior at nearby Gibraltar High, in Fish Creek.

Will we ever forget the fun of our winter fellowship? When we had outings for our church group, we included all the other young people in town. Periodically, there would be ice-skating or sledding and then a gathering at the parsonage for supper, usually spaghetti.

During much of the winter, the snow would be piled so high we were required to tie ribbons on our car antennas, so the cars could be seen around a corner. One night, as I drove home from a meeting, everything was white, except for one touch of black--a frightened little skunk! He was kind enough to let me pass.

Summers found us a beehive of activity. Dozens of college kids came to work in shops, hotels, and restaurants. The population zoomed from 221 to ten times that number. All children who were old enough worked. David had a college-student assistant to help with the young people's program.

Gwen was just twelve when we arrived, but was immediately employed to baby-sit while a mother worked. The grandparents ran the town grocery, so they could keep an eye on things but couldn't take full responsibility. Barbara worked in a gift shop. I loved all the action.

In 1962, as the grand finale for the summer's youth program, a large ferryboat was engaged to take the young people on an outing. The speaker was one of our ministers who had miraculously escaped from the Ukraine. After describing his incredible release from tyranny, he challenged all two-hundred young people to dedicate themselves to fight against anti-Christ Communism. David made a sincere vow to do so--a vow he would never forget.

Often folks from our churches to the south came up for a picnic in the State Park. En route home, they would stop in our home to visit. One Saturday, as I dropped by our local grocery, I debated getting a head of lettuce. *Nobody's coming this weekend; I think I'll skip it,* I concluded. That Sunday evening, we ended up with a record number of dinner guests--several dozen, as I recall. Since all shared their picnic leftovers, it worked out fine, lettuce or no lettuce.

One morning when I woke up, the fresh cold air coming through the open window suddenly made me aware fall had arrived. It was the day after Labor Day, and we had been busy winding up summer activities.

"Goodness, David! I have a problem. Thursday morning we have Circle, and I have nothing to wear." After our return from Nicaragua, the priorities for clothing went to David and the girls, then the baby, and finally me. I had plenty of summer clothes, but nothing suitable for fall meetings.

There seemed no choice but to drive twenty-seven miles to Sturgeon Bay and buy a dress. I hated to take the time, and our poor savings account--after we had purchased a car, clothes, furniture, and all it took to get settled--didn't need one more deduction. Even if I *made* the dress, it would still mean a trip for material and hardly enough time to do it up.

"I'm willing to take you shopping if you want to go," David said.

A huge wash was waiting, and as I plowed into the morning's work I kept thinking and praying about the matter. With the baby in the playpen, I made trip after trip to the basement, where my old Maytag wringer-type washer did six or seven loads. All had to be lugged upstairs and outside to be hung on the line. Continually, I was bringing up the dress problem to the Lord. Part of my quandary was deciding what type of dress would fill in best for many different occasions.

"Do you know anything about that brown bag I saw on the coffee table?" I asked David at lunch.

"Oh, I forgot to tell you. When I went to the post office, I saw Verna and she gave it to me. Said something about Betty having gained weight so she couldn't wear it anymore. She thought maybe you could use it; it was much too good for rummage."

I rushed in, opened the bag--and there it was! The perfect dress. A basic black, considered essential to every wardrobe. It was dressy with pearls or sporty with a scarf. Perfect style, perfect fit! I was aghast. "Lord, You are tops in women's fashions!" I exclaimed.

In the months following, that dress served for many occasions. At one gathering, Betty sidled up to Verna and said, "I wonder what Peggy would have worn if I hadn't gained weight!"

Truly, the Lord's provision came in many ways.

Barbara was about ready for college. We wanted a Christian campus and felt Wheaton College would be the best. When her credentials were submitted, we were given small hope. Many more applications were coming in than they could accept, and because the American School in Managua met for half-days only, Barbara had very few extracurricular activities to report. She had qualified as a National Merit Scholarship semifinalist, but grades were only a third of the consideration. "You can fill out an application, but I can't offer much hope," the Director of Admissions warned.

We based our perseverance on the promise in Psalms 84:11: "No good thing will he withhold from them that walk uprightly."

The Lord sovereignly designed Barbara's senior year in high school. She had the leading role in *The Solid Gold Cadillac* and solo parts in all concerts. She was elected to membership in the National Honor Society, was salutatorian of her class, and received the Danforth award, given for leadership and character.

"Lord, as much as we want her accepted at Wheaton, please don't let her be unless You and we can handle the finances," we prayed. The cost per year was $2500, while our salary was $3600! We had sold the cottage at the seashore, and payments on the mortgage gave us a small monthly supplement--but our budget was still tight.

Eventually Barbara was accepted. With grants, scholarships, winter jobs, summer work, her savings, and some help from us, she completed four years. All her experiences were grist for the mill and developed the resourcefulness and character she would need for her life of full-time service for the Lord.

October 1, 1962, Ann's third birthday, proved to be a red-letter day for her and for me. Having been spoiled by two adoring older sisters, not to mention two doting parents, she had begun throwing temper tantrums--an act of defiance her sisters would never have dared to indulge in.

"We must pray about this," I had confided to David. "If she keeps on, we're headed for problems." We prayed.

Sitting in her high chair at lunch on her birthday, Ann created a scene. David took her to the living room, spanked her, and put her to bed. After our Bible reading, he suggested I check on her. Going up the stairs, I prayed, "Lord, please help me handle this."

Ann was sitting up in bed, still sniffling.

"You were a very bad girl, weren't you?" I asked.

"Y-yes," she half-sobbed.

"You made Daddy feel bad, didn't you?" They were close, and she hated to disappoint him.

"Y-yes."

"Do you like living like this?"

She shook her head. "No."

"Would you like to ask Jesus to forgive you? Then you can invite Him into your heart, and He will live there and help you be a good girl."

"Yes," she nodded.

She prayed after me in total sincerity, truly with a humble and a contrite heart. That was her last tantrum. And so it was that my own daughter was the first soul I led to Jesus.

The spiritual pluses of David's two-and-a-half-year pastorate in Ephraim were many. A new friend from Texas who summered in Ephraim had been a born-again Christian for years. He saw in us two hungry young people who needed training in the Word. Whenever his schedule and ours permitted, he would come to our home for an hour of Bible study. In April of 1961, he brought Arnold Pent, who had been his classmate at Wheaton College, to visit in Ephraim for several weeks. Arnold and his family stayed next door in the Anderson Hotel.

The Pent family read the Bible three times a day. After each meal, they read three chapters and had prayer. The children were a storehouse of biblical knowledge. One of the older boys could finish any verse in the New Testament that our young people started.

After they left, David announced, "I think we could develop their reading habit. Let's cancel the *Chicago Tribune* and try it."

At first, it took eight months to read through the entire Bible; but within a few years we stepped it up to six months. So far, we have gone through the Word well over fifty times.

David and Jim Campbell, a Baptist minister, got together each morning at six to pray for revival. When the snow was frozen like ice, they slipped and slid back and forth to his church or ours as they alternated meeting places. A time or two, we overslept and awakened to snowballs hitting our windowpane.

One day, Jim invited David to go with him to a meeting of the Full Gospel Businessmen's Fellowship in Green Lake, Wisconsin. My husband came home joyous and beaming. I was so happy he had had such a great time--until I got details.

"You never saw anything like it," he said. "There was such love, and joy, and praise. We lifted our hands and sang. Then I prayed and asked for the baptism in the Holy Spirit. I received it, and I speak in tongues!"

"You *what*?" I asked, horrified.

"Speak in tongues," he repeated. Just what I thought he had said.

I knew nothing of this move of God and really didn't care to learn about it. I also knew nothing of the man's being head of the family.

"Well, I don't want any of that in *my* house," was my reaction. For the first time, I knew what it meant to have a skeleton in the closet. I confided the terrible fact to no one. David honored my request and used his prayer language only in private. But he couldn't hide his new boldness.

13--Poetry and Power

Ever since David and I had gotten saved, we had known we were in spiritual warfare. Though most church members instinctively know Bible preaching is right, there's always a vocal minority who want liberal preaching. When the leaders of the opposition are strong, they stir up so much trouble they seem like a majority.

One such leader was on David's Board of Elders. He complained weekly, we supposed, to our district president. Finally there was to be a showdown. The district president--a college mate of my brother and at one time a guest in our home--was to come and meet with David and the joint boards of our church.

We had gone to Youngstown, Ohio, over the weekend for the wedding of David's sister Florence to Bill Daggett. The meeting was scheduled for Monday evening. When we returned from our 450-mile trip, we found a note on the door.

"Have changed plans. No meeting tonight. Instead, I'll come in the morning and meet with the two of you." It was signed by the district president.

As the three of us gathered in our living room the next morning, David explained how he had found Jesus in a personal way on the mission field and could not refrain from making clear the necessity of the new birth for everyone.

The president then turned to me and said, "Well, Peggy, what do you think?"

Only then did I realize the opposition's plan. If they could convince me David's present path was professional suicide, that might be the best way to reach him.

"Well, Brother," I began, praying for the right words, "I, too, found Christ as my Savior in Nicaragua. I stand 100 percent with David in his preaching of the Scriptures as the infallible Word of God. There is nothing else worth telling."

"Do you want me to resign?" I heard David ask. I had a sinking feeling. With Barbara just starting college and our bank account sadly depleted, I wondered what we would do.

To his everlasting credit, the dear man shook his head no, but he advised David to walk as discreetly as possible. Then we parted on a friendly basis.

On the lighter side: The elder who gave David so much trouble was a retired professor with a string of degrees. He wanted social challenge from the pulpit, not biblical preaching. His wife was of the same persuasion.

One lovely fall afternoon, she held a gathering for our local crowd. Vacationers had gone and only the native Ephraimites, plus retirees who had settled there year-round, were left. There must have been fifteen to twenty of us assembled in the newly built town library on the edge of the inlet.

As she was giving us an afternoon of Robert Frost and his poems, my mind was rambling delightfully from the scene of sailboats on the blue waters to the trees of the Peninsula State Park to the south. Many an artist had sketched the spot, and I was tucking it into my memory bank.

Idly I thought, *Let's see--Robert Frost. Oh, yes! In Public Speaking class at Linden Hall, I memorized one of his poems. What was it? Ah, "Mending Wall": "Something there is that doesn't love a wall. / That sends the frozen-ground-swell under it. . . ." I can't remember any more.* My mind went back to the sailboats.

Suddenly I heard our speaker say, "Then we have that charming poem, 'Mending Wall': 'Something there is that doesn't love a wall. . . . '" Pausing, she turned to her colleague, who kept the big book, and said, "See what that next line is."

I couldn't resist. From the back of the room, I filled it in: "'That sends the frozen-ground-swell under it.'"

Silence. David and I were held in such contempt for our belief in the Scriptures that she always preferred to ignore us when possible.

"'That sends the frozen-ground-swell under it,'" her friend read.

"Well, you go to the head of the class," the speaker said to me, and went on with her talk.

O Lord, I love Your sense of humor, I thought, returning to my sailboats.

A year or more after the confrontation, David received a call to a congregation in Winston-Salem, North Carolina. "They want me to fly down and meet with the boards," he told me after reading the letter. "I believe I will. The South is considered the Bible belt. They may be more open."

Upon his return, he was ecstatic. "Every last one of the trustees and the elders, ten or so, was in agreement with our position! They want biblical preaching, and I have accepted the call." The fifty-five-percent raise in salary was not a factor in his decision. I wondered how one spent so much money.

What mixed feelings I had in leaving one of God's choicest spots, and many very dear people! I would never forget the beautiful snows, the one-room schoolhouse with its tennis court watered down in winter for an ice-skating rink, the PTA socials that involved the whole community, the long, slow, gorgeous winter sunsets shimmering on the ice. . . .

The girls had memories for a lifetime too. There was the winter morning when the thermometer registered twenty-three degrees below zero. We could have driven Gwen to school, but it was sunny with no wind.

"Let's do you up real warm," I said to her. "Cover everything but your eyes. When you have grandchildren, you can tell them you walked to a one-room schoolhouse when it was twenty-three degrees below zero."

That afternoon when she returned, her first words were, "Well, I lost my claim to fame. Mr. Statham picked me up."

Then there was the night Barbara came home for Christmas vacation, riding on the bus from Wheaton. A soft, gentle snow had been falling for hours. After dinner, we went out walking and enjoyed one of the most beautiful nights of our life. When the bus came, around midnight, the dear Christian brother who drove it brought Barbara right to our door.

A week before we left Ephraim, God granted David his first experience with miraculous healing. Donna, a member of our church, was going blind at a rapid rate because of diabetes. Since she needed transportation to her eye specialist in Green Lake, we would often take her. On one occasion, we were able to talk privately with Dr. Hitch, her ophthalmologist.

"What are her chances for recovery?" we asked.

"None," he replied. "There is no way to reverse the loss of sight. My objective is to hold what she has as long as possible."

Although David had received the baptism in the Holy Spirit, he had had no follow-up teaching. Donna, however, had a Pentecostal background.

One day, she boldly declared, "David, the Bible says the sick are to call for the elders of the church to anoint them with oil and pray. If you would do that, I believe the Lord would heal my eyes."

Such a thought had never occurred to him. Not wanting to be found lacking in the faith department, he asked his Baptist-minister prayer partner, Jim Campbell, to go with him. Following the instructions given in James 5:15, they anointed Donna with oil and prayed.

At Donna's next appointment with Dr. Hitch, in February, no spectacular change was noted. When she took her eye test in May, however, the nurse rushed for the doctor. He repeated the examination.

"I don't understand this," he told Donna. "On our records, you are listed as legally blind, with ninety percent of your sight gone. Yet today you have forty percent sight in one eye and sixty percent in the other! It's unbelievable." (She had lost the ninety percent in about two years.)

Donna asked the Lord to please let her see well enough to get around, and to read her large-print Bible, as long as she lived. For her remaining thirteen years, the Lord did just that. Her daughter told me at her funeral that she lost sight entirely on her deathbed. When she awoke in glory, she had twenty-twenty vision and still does!

One final note about leaving Ephraim: David was to preach his last sermon on Sunday morning, December 30, 1962. Then we would have dinner with the Wilson family and be on our way. The van had taken our personal possessions on Wednesday, leaving us to get by on the church's items and giving me three days for a thorough cleaning of the large, comfortable parsonage.

By Saturday afternoon, everything was sparkling except for the carpets and the wood and linoleum floors. We had been invited out for meals every day, and each time had stayed to visit. David was totally occupied in the office. I was on my own. I wasn't going to make it.

"Lord, You're going to have to pull one of Your fast ones," I told Him late Saturday afternoon. "I'll never get these floors done by midnight."

The doorbell rang, and Shirley Olsen was there. Coming in, she said, "I didn't plan to stop. I know you're busy. It just seemed I was to come and ask if there is anything I can do for you."

"No, thanks," I told her. "I'm down to floors."

She was thoughtful for a moment, then said, "We have the most wonderful floor-polisher and carpet-cleaner. Why don't we get together, after our children and yours have gone to bed, and have a floor party? I'll bring my husband along."

After we had moved, a trustee sent word that he had never seen a cleaner house and couldn't imagine how we moved out leaving it so immaculate. I'm not an A+ housekeeper, but I tried to leave each parsonage in mint condition. That time, however, without God-given help, I'd never have made it.

It took about five years for me to crystallize the changes my surrender to Christ had brought to my thinking:

1. A burden for the lost had become top priority. I saw friends and loved ones as in a burning building. If they weren't warned, many would surely perish. Before my conversion, I saw only possibilities for

church membership. When a new member joined the church, we hoped they'd be steady, good givers, and bring in others. Before, I could never understand stories of folks excited about witnessing to strangers they'd never see again. Now, I was one of those excited, witnessing folks.

2. I recognized the Bible is infallible. I no longer agreed with the "scholars" that this and that part of Scripture wasn't as it seemed. Security came from knowing that the answer to every question or situation was to be found in the Word. What a relief that such decisions were no longer mine to make. What is truth? "Thy word is truth" (John 17:17). That settled it.

3. Talking about Jesus came naturally. Before my conversion, I rarely named His Name. Now that He was uppermost in my thoughts and activities, His Name came up continually. I wasn't like four-year-old Richard in our student pastorate. As time for Bible school rolled around, he announced he wouldn't be going. When his mother asked why, his answer was simple: "Well, it's about Jesus, and I know all about Him!"

4. I wanted my whole life to shape up. I re-examined it to see if anything needed correction. The one thing that came to mind was something I hadn't thought of for twenty years. During the year I wrote for the *Sunday News*, I had bought a friend's nontransferable bus pass every Saturday afternoon, thus saving us both a small amount of money. After coming to the Lord, I sent twenty dollars to the bus company, to repay with interest the amount I had shortchanged them twenty years earlier.

5. Christianity replaced "churchianity." Previously, the absence of Jesus in my life had left a void I mistakenly filled with love for my denomination.

6. Heaven became real. I loved to read the accounts of folks who had died for a few minutes and had had a brief glimpse of heaven. All were loath to return to earth. I saw clearly I am a pilgrim here. Death, which had held such horrors for me as a child, was now seen as an inviting entrance to an unbelievably beautiful place where one would always be with Jesus.

7. I wanted revival! David and I soaked up all obtainable reading material that described a move of God. Every Christmas and birthday when the girls or I asked David what he wanted, the answer was always the same: "A Holy Ghost, heaven-sent, repentance-producing revival." That's what I wanted too.

8. Perhaps the greatest realization was that the church had failed to warn us. Nobody had ever made it clear to me that, unless I was truly born again, I would not get to heaven. In mainline church circles, hell had been largely a joke. Now I found my Bible spoke of hell and the lake of fire more than fifty times.

   If a doctor makes a grievous error, he may be sued. I half-jokingly said the mainline churches should be sued. But it wasn't funny. When folks slip away in death and learn the truth as soon as their spirits leave their bodies, it is too late. Thus, the liberal pastors seemingly get away with their deception. They will, of course, have to answer at the judgment throne, but that's small comfort to the condemned parishioners who trusted their pastors.

In short, everything had changed. The old Peggy was gone. The new one was alive in Christ. David and I both knew now what we were to do: win souls.

"We are hoping you will take the senior-high Sunday-school class," greeted me as soon as we were settled. I accepted the challenge eagerly. Now that I was born again and knew Jesus personally, I welcomed the ideal platform for telling others the good news.

Of the twenty or so in the class, all were respectful and a pleasure to teach--except for two boys. They were very bright and considered themselves much too enlightened for my beliefs about the Bible and its inerrancy. Their harassment was continual, and I believe it was as unpleasant to the class as it was for me.

One morning the boys' harassment seemed to climax. I went home after church and threw myself down beside the couch. "Lord, You know I'm no match for those boys. They are questioning Your Word, and I am asking You to handle it."

In our Bible study two days later, David and I were reading about the children of Israel and how they were fed in the wilderness. We stopped to discuss how amazing it was that five days a week the manna rotted in twenty-four hours, but the manna gathered on the sixth day was good for forty-eight hours.

Sunday, as soon as the opening prayer was over, the more vocal of the two boys announced loudly, "Ah, we don't believe so different from you. We just think there is a logical explanation for things. For instance, did you know they've discovered an insect that secretes a white fluid that was probably the manna used to feed the children of Israel?"

"Praise the Lord!" I answered. "What a God! He can create an insect that secretes a very talented white fluid. Five days of the week it spoils after twenty-four hours, but on the sixth day it lasts forty-eight hours!"

His jaw dropped. He had no answer. He left the church, and without his influence his buddy gave no further trouble. I was thankful the Lord had come to my rescue.

The Lord had lessons for me continually. Even though I had read many times in Ephesians 5 that wives should be submissive to their husbands, it had never really sunk in--nor had I ever heard any teaching on the subject. When it came to decisions in the home, I thought my ideas were as good as David's. In fact, on occasion I thought they were better.

"Would you believe, three years have rolled around and it's time to renew the insurance on our household property?" I said to David one evening. He was on the other side of the newspaper, and I expected no comment; I was only thinking out loud.

"Just a minute," he said, dropping his paper momentarily. "I'd rather trust the Lord and give that money to missions."

"Oh, no!" I groaned. "Have you any idea what all we'd have to replace in case of a fire? Twenty-five years' accumulation is no small matter."

"Just the same, I'd rather trust the Lord," he repeated.

Regretting I had opened my mouth, I debated what to do. *If I go ahead and write the check, he'll never notice,* I thought to myself. Taking the checkbook and putting pen to paper, I was about to write a check to the insurance company when I thought better of it. No, I couldn't go against David's will. I wouldn't write it.

Now it so happened we had a loose brick in our fireplace. Periodically, I'd express concern about it. We had been given a large load of wood by one of our church members. Each afternoon when David returned from calling, I tried to have a fire going, if it was cold enough, and soft inspirational music on the record player. The more difficult his day had been, the more I wanted home to be a pleasant refuge for him. (Though most of the board members still agreed with David's stand on the inerrancy of the Bible, some women in the church were vigorously opposing him.)

One evening during choir practice, several non-singing spouses were gathered around our fireplace. One of the men, James, was a city fireman, and I asked him about the loose brick. He didn't seem too concerned, so I breathed a little easier. The next morning, however, I happened to drive by the fire station. James saw me and flagged me down.

"Peggy, that house we lost last night had the same problem with the fireplace as yours has. I'm sending the inspector out this afternoon."

By the time the firemen came, I had cleaned the fireplace thoroughly, and it looked spotless. The men looked it over carefully and removed the loose brick.

"Lady, you haven't had any fires in this lately, have you?" the inspector asked.

I thought I'd spare him the gruesome details and not say, "Yes, every day and a big one Sunday for Open House," so I just said yes.

His next words were, "There's no way you could have used this and not had a fire."

As the three of us stood facing the fireplace, the Lord spoke distinctly to my spirit: *If you had sent that check, I'd have let it burn.*

For me, this principle was my own personal woman's liberation. No longer did I have to re-evaluate David's decisions and decide for myself if they were right. Unless a red light went on in my spirit, there was no problem. When I needed advice on a matter, I would first ask the Lord to guide David, as the priest in our home; then I would present the facts to him.

Peggy Jones

Soon after the Lord had driven this point home to me, I had occasion to know a decision of David's was wrong. Rather than challenge it, as I would have done previously, I quietly told the Lord I would follow my husband's directions and trust Him to show David his decision wasn't wise. I forget the details, but I can never forget my awe at seeing the Lord shift the situation and make David's wisdom come out right. This experience confirmed my earlier lesson.

The Lord in His sovereignty has made the men to see the forest, while we women see the trees. Therefore, His divine order of having children submit to parents, wives to husbands, and husbands to the Lord is ideal for all concerned. We have observed seemingly impossible husbands shape up when the wife honors this position.

An exception, we feel, should be made with wife-abusers. We never advise any woman to continue in a dangerous relationship, but rather to leave her husband and let the Lord work and guide.

In our student pastorate, I was chatting with the wife of one of our members, who was of another denomination. We discussed what tithing meant. I explained, "In your case, you could give five percent to your church, and your husband could give five percent to his. After she had thought it over, she concluded, "Oh, we couldn't do that! My husband makes too much."

Ever since our marriage, David and I had tithed all our income, including gifts; but we still had lessons to learn. We once attended a Bible conference for which no charge was made and no collections were taken. We figured what our participation had probably cost, and placed that amount in a box provided for that purpose. A missionary gave an outstanding message the last evening, but again no offering was taken, and it didn't occur to us to give anything.

As we were driving home with one of our members, Mrs. Robertson, she was describing her enthusiasm about the mission talk the night before. "First, I wanted to give a dollar or two," she said. "Then I wanted to give all the cash I had. When he finished, I was ready to give the money I had put aside to pay the electric bill!"

Sitting in the back seat, I pondered the fact we had given nothing above costs. *"If you don't give, I'll take it,"* a Voice seemed to say.

How silly! I thought. *Imagine the Lord taking away if you don't give!* With that, I dismissed it.

The next day, David went on an errand downtown. We had only a twenty-dollar bill. When he returned, I asked for ten dollars to shop. Opening his wallet, he found the parking-lot attendant had cheated him of ten dollars. We laughed as I told him the message I had received: *"If you don't give it, I'll take it."*

I promptly wrote out a check for the missionary and told him the story, knowing he would enjoy it. Within a week, a very odd thing happened. An extra twenty dollars turned up in David's wallet. We were so pressed for cash that it couldn't have been an oversight. I can't explain it; I'm simply reporting a fact.

Even in the Bible belt, the influence of liberals was growing. As with the church in Ephraim, a small but vocal minority fought David's Bible-believing stance by every possible means. After three years, we sensed a change was inevitable.

David and I had often discussed what the Lord might want of us. There were two choices for a minister who had had a born-again experience. Either he could stay in the church, compromising to an acceptable degree and trying to work for good in the denominational framework, or he could quietly withdraw and go elsewhere. For almost ten years, we had done the former.

David had tried on the synod floor to convince the delegates to leave the liberal World and National Councils of Churches. But odds were against him.

Within our own congregations, we had felt good about the young people we led to the Lord. But as long as they were part of the denomination, it was an uphill battle. I could understand when a born-again pastor concerned with increasing liberalism in the church confided, "We're not in a denomination; we're in an abomination." Examples were all around us.

One young boy, newly saved, went happily off to church camp. But he returned with a wounded spirit.

"Preacher, when I told them I was born again, they laughed at me, and one of the ministers said, 'We don't believe that old-fashioned way anymore.'"

One of our dear girls, daughter of an elder, asked the Lord into her heart and had a genuine conversion. She wanted to read her Bible, but it so upset her folks, who ridiculed her and forbade it, that she had to read with a flashlight under the covers at night. Worse than that, any young man who was drawn to the ministry and attended seminary could have the Spirit within him quenched, and graduate spiritually bankrupt.

The answer for us seemed to be not to compromise any longer. The option of going elsewhere and getting lost was apparently our only alternative. After all, David could always return to teaching, I figured.

As I was turning the fried potatoes for our supper on the evening of March 26, 1966, David came to the kitchen door, Bible in hand.

"We must leave the church, but we are to stay in the city," he announced.

"Go on!" I answered. "I've been through that Bible, and nowhere does it mention Winston-Salem."

"Listen to what He told me," David went on. "I was returning from calling, and two of our widows were chatting in front of the drugstore. As I approached, they said, 'Pastor, we've just been talking about our widow's mite going to help Communist causes through the Councils of Churches, and we don't like it. What are you going to do?'

"I went to the church study, fell to my knees at my desk, and cried out to the Lord. Then I opened the Bible, and this is what I read:

> *Therefore, thou son of man, prepare thee stuff for removing, and remove by day in their sight; and thou shalt remove from thy place to another place in their sight: it may be they will consider, though they be a rebellious house.*
>
> (Ezekiel 12:3, emphasis added)

"See, it's repeated twice: we must remove but stay 'in their sight.' We can't leave town."

What an assignment! As the days went by, we began cleaning out the garage and attic, awaiting our marching orders.

Once, while washing the luncheon dishes, I was overwhelmed. I could take the loss of congregation, parsonage, hospitalization, salary, pension--all the security we had had. We had long ago determined never to let finances interfere with our ministry. I could trust the Lord for that, but I could hardly bear to think of facing the disapproval of my family and losing our friends in the ministry and the church.

For some years, we had sensed we'd have to leave the denomination some day. I had made two requests of the Lord. First, I didn't want such a painful break while Mother was living. But just that April, she had remarried in a lovely little ceremony by our fireplace. Now she lived in West Virginia and therefore wouldn't feel our action so keenly.

Peggy Jones

The second request was that it not be while Gwen was home to be torn from her friends in the church she dearly loved. Now she was a freshman at Covenant College in Lookout Mountain, Tennessee. (Barbara had graduated from Wheaton and was teaching Bible in Giles County, Virginia.) So the Lord had honored my two requests, and I couldn't ask for more.

Still, standing at the sink, I panicked momentarily.

"Go in and find how Peter walked on the water," the Lord said.

Barely taking time to dry my hands, I rushed into the living room and grabbed the Bible off the coffee table. I quickly thumbed through the concordance, breathless to find the Lord's answer for me.

I found it in Matthew 14:30,31. After Jesus had walked on the water, Peter asked that He bid him walk on the water too. As he started to walk,

> *he saw the wind boisterous, he was afraid; and beginning to sink, he cried, saying, Lord, save me. And immediately Jesus stretched forth his hand, and caught him, and said unto him, O thou of little faith, wherefore didst thou doubt?*

I felt a real peace. If I could keep my eyes on Jesus and not on the circumstances, I too would "walk on the water," and He would bring me through.

After the word given in late March to prepare for a move, we heard nothing further from the Lord for months. In November, we attended our denominational young-adult rally. Such risque things were said that we and our dear people blushed with shame. We had over forty members in attendance--the largest delegation of any congregation. David and I came home heartsick, so burdened for our poor church. Jesus seemed not to be at all in the thoughts of the people. David said, "Now is the time. We are to leave."

Without saying anything to anyone, we rented a house and began preparing it for services. January 1 happened to be on a Sunday. We decided to announce then that we were leaving on the fifteenth. Before making the announcement, we would have a blessed holiday together and one last grand Open House for all the church's four-hundred members.

Our four years with this congregation had gone fast and, aside from the vocal liberal minority, they had been blessed in every way. We were continually adding members, seeing the sick healed, folks' lives changed, helping the children learn the Word, and being busy about the Kingdom business in general.

However, like Moses, we did not feel equal to the task now assigned us: that of taking a public stand in opposition to the liberal trend of our denomination. Privately I had begged the Lord to give this assignment to another couple, friends of ours, who had more ability all around. I wanted to support them. This sense of inferiority on my part was weighing heavily on my heart. Then the Lord gave me help through an acted-out parable.

Before the holidays, Gwen had written that she must have a housecoat of winter weight at college. In all our upheaval, her need had completely slipped my mind. On Christmas morning, when gifts were opened and there was no robe, she approached me reluctantly.

"Mother, I'm sorry, but I really must have a warm housecoat. The girls all study in them every evening, and mine is too lightweight."

"Honey, we'll go to town tomorrow morning," I promised. "I'm sorry I forgot all about it." In my heart, I hoped for a good buy. Our uncertain future didn't warrant any further purchases.

Linden Hall, Lititz, PA. Founded 1746.
Included a junior college, 1935-59.

Picture taken at the time of our wedding.

Morgan Co-op. Dining hall where David and I met. Dormitory upstairs.

The Swiftwater Inn, since 1778
Swiftwater, Pennsylvania

Old Windmill at Water Mill
Built in 1800
South Fork, Long Island

John Howard Payne's "Home Sweet Home"
Built 1660, East Hampton, Long Island

Home of Albert Einstein
Princeton, New Jersey.

Montauk Point Lighthouse, built in 1795
South Fork, Long Island

Notepaper of historic and picturesque scenes.
Our means of livelihood through seminary.

Gwen, Peggy, Barbara, David -
on Long Island before seminary

Barbara and Gwen

Mountainview, place of David's student pastorate.
Hellertown, PA.

Cottage on Atlantic Avenue, Beach Haven, NJ,
which we built but never used.

Family on leaving for Nicaragua

Map of Nicaragua, Central America.

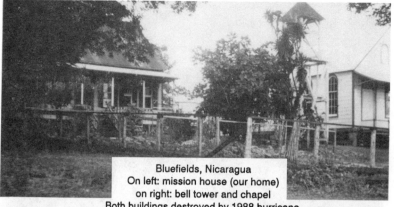

Bluefields, Nicaragua
On left: mission house (our home)
on right: bell tower and chapel
Both buildings destroyed by 1988 hurricane.

Central Church, Bluefields
Communications leaving a communion service.

Christian Endeavor group
about to leave on a banana barge
for a mission trip up the Escondido River

Typical meeting at an isolated farmhouse.
Steadman Bent preaching.

Gwen and Barbara, Managua 1957.

Camp Bethlehem, Managua, 1959

Family in the Ephraim parsonage 1960

Ann as a schoolgirl

Ephraim, Wisconsin, the Cape Cod of the midwest.
White building on the right is the parsonage.

Our first "house church" in Winston-Salem.

Our second "house church,"
Vest Mill Road, Winston-Salem,
where over 1500 meetings
were held, 1971-79.

Gwen, David, Ann, Peggy, and Barbara
during house ministry days in Winston-Salem, NC

David leading service in our home
Vest Mill Road, Winston-Salem, NC

Tour group and bus friends at Upper Room, Jerusalem,
1974 First World Conference on the Holy Spirit.

Gwen and David
on Sea of Galilee

Nancy, a friend, Ann, Gwen, Peggy, and Barbara
on Mount of Olives, Jerusalem.

David and Carl, Helsinki,
minutes after Carol accepted the Lord.

David and Carl at our ship
as we were about to leave

Little housemaid at the Sheraton in Brussels,
receiving her New Testament.

David at Kukenoff Gardens,
Holland, spring 1976

Peggy in front of the watch shop
of Corrie ten Boom"s family.

Baptisms in River Jordan.

Our first two grandchildren each with
Jesus in his heart at age 2 or 3:
Peggy with Victor Hanger.
David with David Hanger.

David receiving the president's award
from Dr. Pat Robertson.

David, minister to guests at 700 club,
in lobby of headquarters.

Peggy, secretary to counselors, on
mezzanine of Omni Hotel, Norfolk,
for a Partners' Seminar.

Our retirement "dream house," Lititz, PA.

Barbara, before her wedding, in the courtyard
of the Anglican School, Jerusalem.
Attendants: Linda Jones, Janice Karnis, Simon Karnis.

Ann, my first convert, and
daughter Ashley.

Our last family get-together, a rare occasion.

Mother and her husband, Harry P. Musser on her hundredth birthday celebration in 1985

Ashley, about the time she reported.
"I asked Jesus into my heart.
The angels are happy."

Standing: Richard and Bob Snyder, David
Seated: Peggy, Helen (Bob's wife), Toylee (Richard's wife).

Standing: Bill Daggett, Florence Daggett
Seated: Helen Snyder, Dorothy Honey, Bob Snyder.

Celebrating Mother's 103rd birthday.

First thing in the morning, we went into the city. Scouring the downtown stores, we were saddened to find no robe in her size even remotely attractive. Then we went out to a shopping center. As we entered Thalhimers, our favorite store, there on the rack was her dream--a yellow quilted, trim-waisted, long flowing robe. I held Gwen's coat and purse as she tried it on. It was at least two sizes too small.

"What is that in thine hand?" the Lord spoke to me.

Immediately I knew He was referring to some pieces of soft quilted pastel material Barbara had just picked up out of a bargain barrel. I answered. "Lord, it's four skimpy pieces of material, and it's not enough."

We had one last store to try. Once again, I held Gwen's coat and bag as she tried on a most unattractive robe.

"What is that in thine hand?" He said it again.

"Lord, it's four skimpy pieces of material, and it's not enough."

As I stood there, I received a mute message from the Lord. He showed me exactly how to do it. There were three identical pieces roughly a yard long and fifteen inches wide. The fourth piece was the same length but wider by five inches or so. In a flash, the Lord showed me the large piece was to be the back, two others the sides in front. On the remaining piece, I was to lay yoke front and back pieces of a blouse pattern I had. The balance I would fold over and use for sleeves. The idea was so clearly from the Lord, I purchased lining and buttons, and we headed home.

"Now Lord, You know I'm busy," I told Him. (The house had over twenty windows, all with venetian blinds, that needed a thorough cleaning. We were getting out a mailing of our statement to all two hundred ministers within our denomination, plus our usual Christmas mailing--held until we could tell our news.

There were duties everywhere I looked.) Reluctantly, I added, "I will give one evening to see if this is of You."

One of Gwen's friends dropped by that afternoon as I was carrying my "four skimpy pieces of material" through the living room.

"Look at this, Leslie. Do you think it can be a floor-length robe?"

Looking at them seriously, she answered, "It would be a miracle." I agreed.

At seven o'clock, I laid the material out on the dining-room table. The three pieces went together exactly as the Lord had shown me. Next, I dug out my blouse pattern and marveled that the pattern pieces fit perfectly on the fourth piece of material! Except for the material cut out for the armholes, *there was not a scrap left.* Ruffling I had on hand took care of the collar and edging; and where the sleeves stopped below the elbow, several layers of ruffling filled in.

The clock struck eleven as I folded up the machine. Aside from some handwork, all was finished.

As I lifted the machine from the table, the Lord spoke: *"It is enough."* I knew He was telling me that, just as four skimpy pieces of material were adequate for the needed robe, even so, two most inadequate lives, given to Him, would be enough too. What a strengthening word!

Later, I realized that, when Moses complained of inadequacy, the Lord asked him the same question He had asked me: *"What is that in thine hand?"* (Exodus 4:2).

Gwen wrote back from school, "My robe is the prettiest one in the wing!"

The announcement of our break was every bit as traumatic as I had feared. The media made quite an issue of it, and folks called and came. Of course, the born-again

Christians understood, though some of them felt we should have just quietly left and gone elsewhere. This would have been our preference.

In David's statement, he made it clear that the church no longer accepted the inerrancy of the Scriptures, and most members seemed to know nothing of the necessity to be born again--the only way to get to heaven.

We had always wondered why the church clung so tenaciously to the radical Councils of Churches, since the National Association of Evangelicals (NAE) was closer to the historic theology of our denomination. Then we discovered the reason. The NAE requires belief in the whole Bible as the Word of God, whereas the modern denomination believes the Bible "contains" the Word of God--a very tricky distinction.

Realizing "as goes the church, so goes the nation," we were concerned about the decline in national morality resulting from the church's failure to honor God's word. Though we felt like the little boy with his finger in the dike, we had to contribute what little we could to the solution.

A special evidence of God's adequacy at this time had to do with Ann, our shy little first-grader, who went to school a block away. We had learned to take all matters, great and small, to the Lord in prayer. From the first day of classes, as she left the house each morning, we put our hands on her shoulders and prayed over her: "Lord, make this child a blessing to all she meets. Help her learn quickly and well. Give her favor and keep her in Your care."

Our move within the city meant she would have to change schools. On Friday, her last day, we sent a note informing the teacher that Ann would be transferring as of Monday.

Midmorning, the doorbell rang. It was the principal himself. We invited him in. He got right to the point.

"The teachers are all sorry to lose Ann. As you know, our first grade is the pilot group for the team-teaching program, and teachers from all over the city come to observe. They wondered if you couldn't bring Ann each day for the rest of the year."

We regretted that our unusual circumstances made that option unwise. But the principal's request was the Lord's sign to us that He had heard and answered those daily prayers, another confirmation that His provision was more than enough.

15--How We Got This Way

Unbelief in the pulpit doesn't just happen, we decided. It is Satan's diabolical plan to get into church colleges and seminaries and teach the students not to believe in the Scriptures. By appealing to intellectual pride in saying each person must evaluate the Word for himself or herself, liberal theologians lead the way by implying no scholar could possibly accept the creation "myth," the story of Jonah, and other biblical accounts. If a student, perchance, comes to college or seminary as a born-again Christian, he soon learns to be silent about it.

According to T.W. Litzenberger, *Redbook* magazine some years ago reported the following results from a survey of ministers in training:

Fifty-six percent rejected the Virgin Birth.
Fifty-four percent rejected the bodily resurrection of Jesus Christ.
Seventy-one percent rejected life after death.
Ninety-eight percent rejected Christ's return to earth.[2]

----
2. T. Wilson Litzenberger, *Startling Trends in Our Generation*

If it was this bad in seminaries in the seventies, how much worse it would be today! Generally speaking, the average church member is not aware that his pastor doesn't believe in the inerrancy of the Scriptures. A mainline church seeking a new minister polled 168 of its members to see if they wanted a born-again pastor who accepted the entire Word of God as divinely inspired. One hundred and fifty-six said yes. And this was considered to be a sophisticated congregation.

One small denomination had a reputation for staying true to the Word over the years. David's cousin happened to be on the Board of their seminary. When visiting with him, we asked, "How do you manage to keep your church on target? How does the seminary stay sound?"

"No problem," he answered. "At the first sign that any professor is teaching unbelief, he is dismissed."

In contrast, we were saddened when a brochure arrived announcing an upcoming lecture at one denominational college and seminary. One of the nation's most radical men was the featured speaker. David approached one of the leaders hopefully.

"As equal time to that man's views, I believe I could get _____ _____ for you. He is a fine Christian and knowledgeable about current affairs."

"Oh, my!" was the reply. "We wouldn't touch him with a ten-foot pole."

The solution to their unbelief? Nothing short of a Holy-Ghost, heaven-sent, repentance-producing revival. We believe the latter rain is due to fall. When, by God's sovereign grace, ministers and missionaries get saved-- born again, just as we did--then the pulpits will be aflame again. Sinners will repent, the sick will be

---

(Broadview: Gibbs Publishing 1974) pp. 172,173.

healed, the oppressed will be delivered, and we will all be looking for Jesus' return to take us Home.

What a wonderful day that will be!

Meanwhile, we are called to occupy until he comes. In occupying, we discovered that the Lord majors in real estate. I mean, who else could manage a lovely ranch-style home nestled in the woods, with a little stream trickling by our bedroom window? A full finished basement made an ideal worship center, and a small apartment to the side provided a lavatory and kitchen facilities, plus an office. It opened directly onto the backyard, with no steps to climb. We loved it. We whitewashed the basement walls and hung drapes for a backdrop.

Our little independent church thrived. Blessings abounded as folks were saved, healed, or just nurtured. The young people enjoyed Bible contests and sword drills, and a spirit of excitement permeated our gatherings.

David and I were having our needs met, but our youngest daughter was not. "David, Ann needs friends," I told him one day. "These neighbor girls play together and never invite her."

He said what he usually says: "Let's pray about it." Then he added, "I don't want her to have worldly friends; the Lord can supply a Christian friend."

When I want to take some positive action and my husband takes the prayer route, I sometimes get impatient. "You talk as though one can pull little Christian girls out of a hat," I answered. "I doubt there are any around."

We prayed.

In a few days, Ann happily announced a PTA meeting. The children were invited to come too, so they could take their parents to meet the teachers and see their rooms. I was busy and sorely tempted not to go.

Realizing how Ann had had to adjust to a totally new environment, I felt I owed it to her to go, so I took her to the meeting.

Every face was strange, until the treasurer got up to give his report.

"Ann," I nudged, "I know that man. He befriended the elderly missionary couple who used to live here. They had no kin, and he was like a son to them. We met him briefly once as he was leaving their house. I want to talk to him."

As soon as the meeting adjourned, we lost no time finding Jim Chatman, his wife Miriam, and their daughter Cathy. I might have known: the Lord had set the whole evening up! Cathy and Ann became the best of friends. They shared their Christian books and had many happy hours together. Jim and Miriam both worked, but they had a fine housekeeper. Whenever we had to be away from home after school, Ann was most welcome at Cathy's house--and when we went out of town, she often spent the night with Cathy.

One summer the two of them attended five Vacation Bible Schools together! What better use of time could eight- and nine-year-olds have?

That fall was dry. I frequently looked at the woods to the rear and felt a concern about fire. Then one day it happened.

One of our women was recovering from flu, and David said he thought he would call on her. He had almost closed the door when I called him back.

"I want to send something. Would you mind waiting?"

As I stood stirring my love gift at the stove, my eyes fell naturally on the woods back of our house. Was that smoke? I rushed to the picture window and was horrified to see a grass fire spreading rapidly from our neighbor's yard. I screamed to David and Ann, and we grabbed buckets and brooms and dashed out. For half an hour we worked feverishly--David especially. He was beet-red, out of breath, huffing and puffing as we extinguished the last bit of burning grass. The fire had worked right out to the trees, and was within moments of igniting them.

The neighbor who had started burning trash and forgotten about it was horribly embarrassed. But oh, how I thanked the Lord for not letting David be gone!

One night I woke up, so restless I had to get out of bed-- a rare occurrence for me. Leaving the bedroom, I went through the hall and stood at the kitchen door. Suddenly I saw sparks flying at the window above the sink. I rushed over as they flew again, with three times the intensity, and with a sizzling noise.

Quickly, I yanked the lamp cord from the socket. Water had collected behind the drainboard, and the cord was lying in it. Within seconds, the curtains would have caught fire. The split-second timing of the Lord's alerting me was nothing short of miraculous.

We didn't know it then, but He was about to perform another split-second miracle for us.

A familiar voice on the phone was that of the founder of Joy Ranch Children's Home in Hillsville, Virginia. "Can you pick up the children's choir robes at the airport and bring them when you come up for our Open House tomorrow?"

David was on the Board of the Home, and was delighted to help. Conveniently, Henry and Jewell Masten had invited us for a cookout that night. The airport was just beyond their home.

It was our habit, when visiting Christian friends, to open the Bible and share something. That evening,

David read from Daniel about the three Hebrew children in the fiery furnace. Moments later, Henry, Sammy Everhart, and David drove off in our sturdy Olds on the errand at the airport. We all believed in miracles but didn't dream we would need one so soon.

Darkness had settled by the time they started home. Saturday-night traffic seemed routine for the single-lane road approaching Hastings Hill Crossing. The blinking yellow caution light, double yellow lines for no-passing, and thirty-five-mile speed zone were all there for good reason.

The men's light chatter gave way to horror as they saw twin pairs of headlights at the top of the hill. Someone was speeding to pass a car. A split-second head-on collision loomed. David had time only to gasp, "Jesus!" as he whipped the car onto a steep embankment to escape certain death for all. But not before the young drinking driver raked our car from stem to stern.

Climbing out of our overturned, totaled vehicle, and learning no one in it was hurt, David headed back on shaky legs to find the driver of the other car. Amazingly, he too was unhurt. The Fourth Man had been there, just as surely as He had been in the fiery furnace with Shadrach, Meshach, and Abednego.

After some months, a friend called to tell us a church building nearby was available, along with a parsonage next door. The price was right, and we moved. On the whole, the happiness, validity, and fruits continued. In less than three years, the buildings were over half paid for, without a fund-raising drive or pressure of any sort.

Life had its lighter moments. One morning after the service, several of us got into extended visiting. Ann and her friend, Jennie, ran out of activities to keep themselves amused. Then they spotted the offering plates. Ah, they could help the treasurer! They opened all envelopes, making a neat pile of them, and another pile of the bills they had contained.

Poor Bill, our treasurer! We wished him well as he took the mess home to sort. The girls were disappointed that their "good deed" had met with consternation rather than appreciation. They had only wanted to be helpful. Sometimes our grown-up efforts to be helpful got us in trouble too.

After David added radio programs to his schedule, he found himself getting into real spiritual warfare. No warfare is pleasant, but the alternative of letting Satan forge ahead is even less attractive.

"Just call me Mrs. Jeremiah," I told a friend. As David tackled one problem after another, he had to fast more and more. He lost weight, his collar hung loose, and I wanted to feed him.

One Tuesday noon, after the Bible-study women left the parsonage, I went over to David's study in the church. He had been fasting again, and I could tell he and the Lord had been talking.

"The Lord's been telling me I must take a stand on the forced-school-busing issue. It's not of Him, and He doesn't like it. We are to keep Ann at home."

I realized that could mean jail. By David's manner, I knew he felt he had it clearly from the Lord and would never back down.

Busing in Southern cities was out of all proportion to common sense. Black and white children alike were bused to schools far from home, sometimes up to twelve or fifteen miles. Many black families found the busing as distasteful as the whites. We women at home, in one-car families, had no way to reach our children in case of illness or other emergency. All this to please some liberals, who were using one more means of controlling our most prized possession--our children. Many of *them* sent their children to private schools.

Ann was in sixth grade, and she stayed home. As the matter became publicized, a teacher friend brought us sixth-grade books. Having taught a Calvert home-schooling course in Nicaragua to Barbara and Gwen, I was accustomed to it.

When the matter came to court, the judge ruled David must spend five days in the Forsyth County jail. David felt the Lord said he was not only to abstain from food, but also to do without any liquid during this time. Going without water can be very dangerous to the system. David looked terrible. On the third day of his total fast, authorities summoned a doctor. His decision was that David must drink. But as David obediently approached the water fountain, the Lord reminded him of what He had said. David obeyed God rather than man. On the fourth day, they sent him home, looking as if he had spent months in a concentration camp.

How much good resulted from his witness, accompanied by fasting and prayer, there is no way to know. Soldiers are not informed of all the fruits of their efforts. Just so, in God's army, we are required only to be obedient and to leave the results to Him. After the fast, Ann returned to school.

Even more intolerable than the forced busing was the school's sex-education program shaped by far-left people with apparently no moral standards. One of our church girls was consistently embarrassed by a male teacher of sex education. Clearly, prophets of old would have thundered from pulpits against this so-called education. But liberal ministers held their peace regarding such issues.

After duly protesting in every way we knew, with no response, we transferred Ann to a Christian school.

Only the Lord knows how the unwholesome sex education in public schools has affected poor children who had no choice but to remain there. Witness all the teenage pregnancies since "enlightenment" took over. But no matter how bad things look to the natural eye, we know that we are more than conquerors.

Our independent church was four years old when David decided the congregation was ready to learn about the baptism in the Holy Spirit. He brought in a Pentecostal speaker for a week of services.

In his eagerness to teach about the third Person of the Trinity--such a necessary gift of God through the Lord Jesus Christ--he could have been overzealous. He made several mistakes, and we were told to leave the church.

This was one of the low points of my life. I went through days in a state of shock. But the Lord had a provision for even this. A dear friend, Cathy Jeunnette, would often drive across town for a visit and a word of encouragement.

"Never mind," she kept telling me. "You are on the Lord's side. He never lets us down. If something is taken away, He will replace it with something better. Some day, you'll even be writing a book about all this!"

She was certainly right about the Lord's having better things in store--and about the book, too.

Church by-laws, which David had framed, required a thirty-day notice for dismissal. During those thirty days, we prayed. The word from the Lord was clear: "*They will not succeed.*" This we mistakenly took to mean they would not be able to put us out. Instead of house-hunting, we held nightly prayer meetings for those who wanted to be with us.

As the fourth week rolled around, with no change in the situation, I called thirteen realtors. There were only two houses to rent, and both were small and inadequate.

On the twenty-ninth evening, we saw a newspaper advertisement for the ideal house. Surrounded by woods, on the edge of town, it had space for forty to fifty worshipers, and parking for thirty to forty cars. The owner was puzzled by the previous tenants' leaving so unexpectedly. We weren't. Once again, we had witnessed the Perfect Realtor at work.

As for those who put us out, they did *not* succeed. After a rapid succession of pastors, they gave up and disbanded, leaving the buildings, largely paid for, to another group.

Vengeance is mine, saith the Lord.

16--Welcome, Holy Spirit!

"We will open our home for all who care to come," was the way the *Winston-Salem Journal* quoted David in writing up the latest chapter of our spiritual sojourn. The article went on to say that unstructured services would be held for the sole purpose of praising the Lord and seeking the ministry of the Holy Spirit. For the first time in twenty years of ministry, we were totally free to be led of the Spirit, unhindered by denominational requirements.

A group of Spirit-filled laymen offered to serve as an advisory board in case of any needed correction. This time, we encountered no opposition, as only those led of the Lord attended the services. No offerings were taken, and money was mentioned only if a brother or sister had a need.

Living by faith was exciting. Now I knew for sure that *I* needed the baptism in the Holy Spirit. Jesus made it clear in Luke 24:49, when He admonished: "I send the promise of my Father upon you: but tarry ye in the city of Jerusalem, until ye be endued with power from on high." For years, I had seen the power, peace, and victory the baptism gave the believer and had observed healing miracles and the operation of the gifts of the Spirit in general. Oh, how I wished the church had required us to remain at seminary until we, too, had received the power.

Finally, I was admitting that I needed the power of the Holy Spirit for myself. "Please take me to Dorothy Weymann's," I said to David. Earlier, we had gone to Greensboro to attend some of the Tuesday-evening prayer meetings held in her home.

One morning, after dropping Ann off at her school, we drove to Greensboro. Dorothy's father, the Reverend James Mason, prayed for me, and I received three words in a new prayer language only God could understand. This was my introduction into the charismatic experience. The greatest victory, I suspect, was in my being humble enough to ask for the gift of the Spirit. The Lord was waiting for that. As time went by, I amazed myself with my newfound boldness.

Before long, Barbara and Gwen left their teaching positions in Asheville, North Carolina, and Tallahassee, Florida, and came home to receive the baptism in the Holy Spirit and grow in the Lord with us.

That summer, the Lord gave them a crash course in evangelism. Our friend Dorothy Weymann and her daughter Margaret invited them on a three-week "fishing" trip in Europe. Using Eurail passes and plenty of tracts, they wasted no opportunities. As they entered train compartments, they split up and each one tried to sound out her seat partner. If they sat by someone who seemed open to ministry, they gave Dorothy the high sign. She would quietly swap seats with them and finish the job by the time the train stopped. The girls said Dorothy was a real pro: before the train's next stop, she could cover Genesis to Revelation and invite her seat-mate to receive the Lord and be filled with the Holy Spirit.

The girls were a great blessing to the family, and also to the fellowship. Ann had been alone at home. Now the three rode together to a Christian day school, where Ann studied and her sisters taught. Each had received the baptism and could minister with us, or minister *for* us when we were gone.

Over a period of eight years, we held more than 1500 meetings in our home. Two on Sunday (morning and evening), one on Tuesday morning, and one on Thursday evening. That meant there was a service suitable for any schedule. Those who attended were rich and poor, black and white, young and old, Catholic and Protestant--all happy to be part of such a fellowship. Several times, persons with Jewish and Islamic backgrounds came to worship with us.

There were no boards, no official membership, pledges, or offerings--just a matter of drinking deeply at the spiritual well that never runs dry. The typical order of service was the singing of Scriptures and choruses, Bible study, prayer, and ministry, with all of the spiritual gifts in operation. (See 1 Corinthians 12:8-10.) Each service ended with a chair being placed in the center of the room, where folks with special needs could come to be prayed for and anointed with oil.

Some individuals who had experienced a genuine conversion wanted to be baptized by immersion. Periodically, we would announce a gathering on Sunday afternoon at Lowrey's Lake outside Winston-Salem. There, in a lovely pastoral setting, the new converts would give their testimony and be baptized. Others came to encourage, bless, and sing scriptural choruses.

How exciting it was to watch the Holy Spirit do the works of the Lord! One evening a mother of teenagers came and quietly took everything in. At prayer time she asked us to intercede on behalf of her young son, who was into drugs. She continued coming, and eventually her husband joined her. Soon both were born again and Spirit-filled. They went off to seminary and have been in the pastorate for over ten years. Their sons are now a great blessing to them.

They were one of six or eight couples in our fellowship who went into full-time ministry. No appeals were made; people simply couldn't resist the desire to serve.

Our ministry extended throughout the city. One minister called David the "Chaplain of Winston-Salem." Early on Wednesday mornings, he held weekly meetings at Dee Dennison's home for Thalhimers store employees. On Monday evenings, at the North Carolina School of the Arts, he met with a precious group of students who took a bold stand for the Lord. Students from Wake Forest University and the University of North Carolina at Greensboro periodically made requests for meetings.

Outside Winston-Salem, there were weekly meetings in private homes in Thomasville and Kernersville, and monthly ones in Mt. Airy and Burlington. Occasionally Margaret Jensen would call from Greensboro. "David, Mother would enjoy some fellowship, Bible-reading, and prayer. Can you come over and have lunch?" Mrs. Tweten was every bit as dear as Margaret portrayed her in *First We Have Coffee*. I loved the story of the evening the family had gathered around her bed. In her sweet manner, she said, with eyes twinkling: "Wouldn't this be a lovely time for Jesus to come take me Home? Why don't we have tea while we wait?"

Sometimes the Lord even supplied luxuries during this period. Soon after we had relocated, I drove by

Winston-Salem's finest country club. Situated on a spacious lawn, the stately, pillared, white Southern-style clubhouse looked most inviting.

"Lord," I said aloud, "I'd like to eat there."

Weeks later, a Presbyterian woman received the baptism in the Holy Spirit and began to attend our meetings on a regular basis. Whereas in her former years her life was occupied with cards and social events, now all she wanted was to talk about spiritual things.

One day she said, "I want you to come to the Club as my guests; then we can talk about the Lord at leisure." Thus began what was to become practically a weekly treat. Usually we'd meet for lunch, lingering over our coffee and dessert till the dining room was empty. Waiters and waitresses, even the cook and kitchen help, would seek us out with prayer concerns. One employee prayed the sinner's prayer right beside our table. When Gwen was married, our friend hosted her bridesmaids' luncheon in the club's private dining room. The next year, she arranged a farewell dinner for us in the same dining room.

This friend had a ministry to the "up and outers." The salvation of her contemporaries became a matter of utmost concern to her. When she felt the leading of the Lord, she would make an appointment, call David, and together they would go and present the Gospel to one of her friends. Some received Christ, some rejected Him. The woman is in Glory now, but she didn't go empty-handed.

Typical of the Spirit's operation was an incident that happened with our Ann.

Vicki, one of our single mothers, was desperate for a sitter for her four children. She worked in the office of her apartment complex and was only a minute or two away from home. She asked Ann, who was only twelve, to try taking care of her children during the summer.

All went well with the three girls, but the boy was older, more venturesome, and daring. Ann was always afraid he would get hurt. As she went into her second week on the job, she asked for special prayer Sunday evening. A prophecy was given: "There will be an emergency, but if you pray in tongues it will work out all right."

Monday morning found Ann and her young charges at the pool. The lifeguard on duty was a middle-aged woman dressed in casual clothes, obviously confident her services in the water wouldn't be needed. Suddenly the swimmers called her attention to a boy's body lying on the bottom of the pool. Nobody knew how long he had been under water.

The lifeguard dived in immediately, clothes and all, and brought the boy up. She worked over him feverishly while someone raced to call the emergency squad. Remembering the prophecy, Ann prayed quietly but frantically in her prayer language. The boy was rushed to the hospital. The evening paper reported he was revived and went home without any ill effects.

One can't claim anything, but we knew Ann's prayers hadn't hurt. And after that scare, her male charge obeyed beautifully.

One day at an evangelistic rally in the city auditorium, the speaker, Kenneth Copeland, suddenly stopped in mid-sentence.

"You there in the navy dress and white collar--stand!" he said. One of our faithfuls, a young single mother, stood to her feet.

Then he spoke this prophetic word: "You will go to other countries far from here to spread the Gospel."

Kenneth, you've blown it this time, I said to myself. *There is no way under the shining stars that she can serve overseas.* I knew that this dear mother of two young boys lived on welfare in a basement apartment and was struggling just to keep going.

Soon afterward, she learned the local black university was required by law to enroll whites. Scholarship funds were available to her, and she enrolled and got her degree. Then she signed up with Youth with a Mission, went to Hawaii for training, then on to Japan and South America to do puppet work.

During service one day the phone rang. The son of a couple in our congregation was being taken to the hospital. Would I please tell them? As I reported the fact, I heard myself add, "But he's going to be all right. There is no need for you to go." The son was a grown man with a wife and child.

The "word of knowledge," which I had been given, one of the gifts of the Spirit, was new to the young man's parents, and naturally they were concerned. They hastened from the room in panic. Soon afterward, they returned, reporting that their son had been dismissed on arrival at the hospital and had already gone home.

Another word of knowledge came one Sunday evening at prayer time after I sat in the prayer chair in the middle of the room. "Please pray for my friend Mary, in Minneapolis," I said. "This week is crucial in her house-hunting. So far, she's not found anything suitable."

After service, David Burr approached me. David was pastor of Winston-Salem's prestigious First Presbyterian Church. He didn't come often to our services but was a blessing to all when he did. He had received the baptism in the Holy Spirit as a young man, though he didn't know what it was until later.

"Your friend will get the house the Lord has for her," he said. "He showed it to me. It's on a corner and on the left."

"Thank you, David. That's good news. I'll write her tonight."

As I wrote, I wondered about "on the left." After all, any house is on the left if you're traveling in the right direction, I reasoned.

Mary's return letter thrilled me. In essence, it said: "The word of knowledge the Lord gave David Burr was the most wonderful reassurance I could have wanted. The realtor refused to sell me anything till I looked at a town house. I felt it was out of my price range but agreed to see it Monday evening. None of the other properties had appealed to me. The minute I walked in, I knew this one was home. Imagine, no snow to shovel or grass to mow! Everything about it is perfect for my needs. It did mean I had to sell some securities. That was my only concern. It all happened so fast, as I had to sign by Wednesday noon. When I came home, there was your letter.

"The house is on a corner and on the left side of a dead-end street! Now I know I will be all right, as the Lord is in it."

Time proved the house to be an excellent investment for her. I loved watching the Lord work all things together for good that way.

One lovely autumn day, friends named Bill and Jonnie invited us to join them for dinner at Greenfield in the mountains and a drive on the Skyline Drive. After stopping at scenic lookouts, we saw it was getting late. At the last vista, we found a couple preparing coffee at their camper as an older woman stood by.

We introduced ourselves. When the elderly woman said she was from Galax, I remembered a young man from there who had left Forsyth Hospital a few weeks earlier. As a hospital volunteer, I had delivered his mail for months and taken a real interest in him.

"Do you by any chance know Joe _____?" I asked. "He was in an accident and spent months in our hospital. I've wondered how he's doing."

"No," the woman said mournfully. "There have been so many accidents. My son was killed in one three weeks ago."

The woman and Jonnie and David walked off. Bill and I stayed with the younger couple, and learned the mother's greatest concern was the question of the young man's salvation.

"My brother was saved as a youth but had back-slidden," the wife said. "He lived forty-five minutes after the accident, but nobody was with him. Mother is so worried, wondering if he had asked forgiveness for his sins. She is inconsolable, fearing he may have gone to hell."

The husband, a husky man in his late forties, added, "I'm in road construction and should be at work. But when I came home for lunch, my wife said maybe it would help if we brought her mother out to see the scenery."

When the others returned, David suggested we form a prayer circle. As we were praying, he got a message in his prayer language along with the interpretation, which he spoke forth: *"Your son is with Me, and when you come to Me, you will see him."*

She'll never understand this, I thought. But the woman opened her eyes a new creation. As we got in the car to leave, she came over, a spring in her step. "Now I have to be getting back to my husband. If you ever get to Galax, be sure to look me up." As we drove off, she waved goodbye.

Indeed, it *had* helped to bring her up to see the scenery.

We also saw physical healings in abundance.

"I want the body to pray for me," our good friend, Rose Hill, said at the close of a Sunday-morning service. "I've had a lump in my breast for some time. I told my daughter, and she's insisting I go to the doctor. But I know Jesus can take care of it."

Pray we did. Vehemently, fervently. Rose had been driving faithfully fifteen miles or so for services and never missed one--not even on Thursday evenings after she'd put in a long day at work.

All day Sunday, I had her on my heart. We couldn't wait to get a report when she returned for the evening service.

She came in beaming. "I checked when I got home, and the lump was still there. I checked again in the afternoon, and it was still there. But when I checked before leaving a short while ago, it was *gone!*"

How we thanked the Lord! That was over a dozen years ago, and there's been no recurrence of the problem.

One man was in the hospital with tuberculosis. David called on him and prayed. Soon he was back at work. Later he told David, "When you put your hand on me that day in the hospital, I felt a charge like electricity go through my body, and I was totally healed." This man worked for years after that, with no further tuberculosis.

Perhaps the most significant healing was that of Jo Johnson. The Lord had healed her of cancer once, but the malignancy recurred, worse than before. She sank slowly until her husband, doctor, and we had all lost faith. But one friend, Sara Shore, had not. She called Jo and asked, "Jo, do you want to die?"

"No, I'd like to raise my children and be with my husband."

"All right. Make up your mind you're not going to die." Sara spoke on in faith--powerful, believing faith.

Peggy Jones

That was more than twelve years ago. We look forward to a Christmas card from Jo and Jim each year.

Occasionally, David and I ministered simultaneously. One afternoon he was ministering to someone in the living room when our friend Elsie was brought for prayer for backache. I invited her to wait in the kitchen where I was working. As Elsie told me how miserable she was, I decided there was no need for her to wait until David was free. She was already seated in a straight-back chair, so I asked her to extend her legs. We had found that legs of unequal length were a frequent cause of back pain. Sure enough, one of Elsie's legs was an inch or more longer than the other. I cupped my hands and held her heels as I prayed. As expected, the shorter leg moved out until both were the same length. And as expected, that ended her back pain.

On another occasion, we had a good laugh when a tall, thin young mother who needed prayer to correct the length of uneven legs said, "Would you mind asking the Lord to shorten the longer leg? He knows I don't need another inch!" To our amazement, He did just that. The skirt patterns she had altered to accommodate her deformity actually had to be *re*-altered.

One day, David himself asked for prayer that his legs be made even. He sat in a straight chair with his legs stretched out in front of him. While the congregation was praying, the shorter leg moved forward an inch or more. David actually heard the squeak of leather as his shoes rubbed together.

Sometimes perfect strangers were brought to our door for ministry. One was a teenaged girl tormented by demons. David ministered to her, and the child left in a peaceful state, but he had had quite a struggle before she was freed from the wild spirit that manifested itself. When I came home, I found the living-room drape down and the drapery rod torn from the wall. Exorcism is a necessary ministry, but not a pleasant one. Fortunately, cases requiring it were rare.

I would be less than honest if I said *everyone* was healed after prayer. In Jesus' day, He healed *all* who came to Him. The late Kathryn Kuhlman asked the Lord for a service where all would be healed. He never granted her request. It remains a mystery why some are healed and some are not, but we give thanks for the miracles the Lord has enabled us to see.

All in all, the seventies were exciting days spiritually. We loved one family's experience, that of Anne and Joe Neel of Burlington, North Carolina. Anne and Joe were typical mainline Christians. Church members all their lives, they never dreamed there was more.

Then--"Mother, I've accepted Jesus and been baptized in the Holy Spirit. I'm so happy!" daughter Dottie reported by phone from Morganton. After some more excited fill-in, the conversation ended.

Anne immediately dialed her other daughter, who lived in Winston-Salem. "Becky, what do you know about the Holy Spirit?" she asked.

"Why nothing, really," she admitted.

"Well, Dottie just called, and she was all excited and so happy. Said she'd just accepted the Lord and been prayed for to receive the Holy Spirit. The way she talked, I figured it was good, so I told her I was happy for her. But I don't know what it's all about."

The more Anne thought it over, the more curious she became. As days went by and her daughter continued walking in joy, she felt sure this was good. Finally, she developed a plan.

"Dottie, how about if you bring several of these Spirit-filled Christians over to the Burlington Country Club? Becky can bring several people from Winston-

Salem, and I'll invite my friends. We'll have lunch in the private dining room, and you can tell us all about it."

The luncheon was a great success. One outcome was that both Anne and Joe were born again and baptized in the Holy Spirit.

This happened about the time of Joe's retirement from his job as chief administrator for the late Senator Everett Jordan's textile plant. The IRS soon checked up on his income-tax return.

"Mr. Neel, how is it you've tripled your giving after retirement? It's usually just the reverse." That gave Joe just the opportunity he wanted to witness to his new life in Christ.

And how about the Neels' friends? Well, they organized a weekly luncheon at a local steak house. It was our privilege to minister there for a time. We understand the meeting is still going strong today.

The Neels used their retirement years to serve the Lord faithfully. They could be found at all special meetings and conferences, and the encouragement they gave to all of us would be impossible to measure.

One afternoon, Anne heard Joe fumbling at his desk. When she went to investigate, she found he had had a stroke and couldn't talk. With her help, Joe made it to his easy chair. Anne immediately rebuked the stroke in the name of Jesus Christ. Then she called their minister.

He prayed and anointed Joe with oil according to James 5:15. After he left, Anne helped Joe get to bed, and then quoted and read Scripture after Scripture to him.

"Now's the time, Joe, for us to prove that our faith in Jesus is real--and powerful." He nodded in agreement.

After three days of Anne's diligence in continually filling his mind and heart with the Word, Joe's speech and side were normal again. An interesting observation Anne made was that, whenever friends called or came in an attitude of unbelief, Joe's symptoms became worse. Conversely, when *believers* inquired or visited, his condition improved. He had several good years before going to be with Jesus, to enjoy the heavenly home prepared for him.

17--The Best Investment

One New Year's Eve, I called Mother in Charleston, West Virginia. She told me their housekeeper had been given time off for the holiday, and she and her husband, Harry Musser, were feeling lonely. She wanted us to come for a visit.

Usually we didn't drive to West Virginia in winter. The round trip was 450 miles, and for my week-long visits every quarter, I used the bus or flew. David and I had anticipated a quiet, leisurely holiday, now the girls were gone.

"Can't you come?" Mother begged.

"Well, if you really need us, I guess we might make the effort," I reluctantly agreed. "The weather is to be clear."

Early on New Year's Day, we bundled up and took off.

"Watch for the first gas station that's open. I didn't know in time to fill up in advance," David said.

At Hillsville, Virginia, we found a station open. A young boy, twelve or thirteen, came to wait on us. He and David talked the entire time the boy was servicing our car. Then they bowed their heads for prayer. David paid for the gas, handed the boy a tract, and returned to the car.

"He just accepted Jesus," was David's happy announcement as we drove away. "He had come to help his grandfather." The Lord had richly rewarded the boy's sweet spirit.

Heady with success, we drove on. The roads were practically empty. Soon we came across a young couple hitchhiking. Though we never pick up anyone, the Lord impressed us to stop this time. The young people were cold and tired, and said they hadn't slept in two nights. Right off, they announced they wanted to sleep.

"Before you do, may we ask if you are Christians?" one of us said.

"No, we're not," was the reply.

David then gave them the simple plan of salvation. They really woke up and showed an amazing interest-- almost as though they knew there had to be more to life than they had found. Just before getting on the turn- pike, David pulled over to the side of the road and led them in the sinner's prayer. They were almost too ex- cited to sleep, but we had a restful ride into Charleston, where we let them off.

Imagine our surprise to find a happy party in progress at the Musser home! Apparently, all of us had forgotten it was a New Year's Day custom for Harry, Jr., his wife Helen, and their family, plus a good friend, Bob Kresge, to come for a football-game party. Since they love the Lord as much as we do, they rejoiced over the account of our profitable journey. We all had a good laugh out of our needless ride to cheer up the lonely.

The next morning, we returned home. Out of seventy-five or so trips to Charleston, that was the only one in which we led a soul to Jesus en route. Obviously, the Lord had arranged the trip.

Our friend, Carlis Fulk, was always a blessing at our meetings. He was pastor of a small rural church up in the Virginia hills, and he invited David to hold a service there one fall evening.

"Come up in the morning," he suggested, "and let me show you around one of the apple orchards." Our friends, Dee and Ralph Dennison, had given us a key to their cottage just off the Blue Ridge Parkway, and we planned to spend the night there after the service.

Arising early on October 31, we made the journey in a little over two hours. After touring the apple orchard and processing plant, we enjoyed many scenic views on our way to the Dennison cottage. We loved that place, especially in fall. It was an old structure, and Dee and Ralph had fixed it up most attractively. It reeked with mountain atmosphere. After a late lunch, we made up the bed and were ready for the evening.

The service went well. When we had said our last goodbye, we headed for the cottage. We had been warned that the stock Halloween prank was to saw trees and fell them across the road. Sure enough, a fallen tree blocked our path. Fortunately, men had already arrived to work on its removal.

We finally settled into our soft, downy mattress around midnight, utterly exhausted. In the stillness, a scurry of little feet could be heard in the loft directly above us.

"What's that?" I asked in alarm.

"Sounds like an animal of some sort," David answered.

"Oh, dear! Who knows how many creatures have taken refuge from the cold since the Dennisons were here? What should we do? I can't sleep in peace, not knowing who or what the enemy is."

"Why don't we take the authority the Lord's given us over the animals?" David suggested. Then he did so: "In the name of Jesus, be gone!"

With that, there was one flurry of running, then quiet. We quickly fell asleep.

In the morning, as we passed the steps leading up to the loft, we saw a dead mouse. He had apparently run over the edge and fallen in a fatal plunge.

If asked to sum up this eight-year period in one word, I believe all five of us would answer: "Happiness." We were serving the Lord, and that always produces joy and satisfaction. Our family life was bliss. The girls never missed a service. After evening meetings, they reappeared in the red-checked granny gowns I had made them and started on schoolwork.

Sunday evenings about ten o'clock, after the last worshiper had left, we took a break together for our favorite time of the week: onion sandwiches around the kitchen table. It was always exciting to review the things the Lord had done that day.

Had we not had these years together, after all of us had received the baptism, we would never have known what the Lord intended family life to be. As Pat Boone described it, the Holy Spirit is the oil in the machinery.

During this eight-year period of total dependence on the Lord, we had no sickness. In fact, the only medication taken by all five of us in 100 months was one aspirin--and that was provided through free samples that had come in the mail. David gave it to Barbara one day after she painfully sprained her ankle.

Although I'd been troubled with various physical problems over the years, I had none for that anointed time. It seemed as though our home and family were under the special care of Jesus. The promise was right there in the Bible:

My son, attend to my words; incline thine ear unto my sayings. Let them not depart from thine eyes; keep them in the midst of thine heart. For

they are life unto those that find them, and health
to all their flesh. (Proverbs 4:20-22)

None of us realized we were in training. David was learning much about ministry, deliverance, faith, healing, and all he was going to need to know. He learned to discern when a cult was manifesting itself in a person. If that person wanted deliverance from an evil spirit, he could minister it. The girls and I were learning to minister too. In addition, I was teaching the girls, just as my mother had taught me, how to live on a little--a handy bit of knowledge for anyone with Christian service in mind.

Folks had learned I wasted nothing. One Saturday evening, a farm family in our fellowship brought us a full bushel of cucumbers. First thing Monday morning, I headed for the country and located a woman who had fresh dill for sale. Next, I rounded up gallon jars. Then I did up the pickles. Family and guests enjoyed their fill of them.

Every fall, we'd get gifts of pumpkins. Aside from pies, I also made them up like mashed potatoes and served them hot as a vegetable. Somehow I don't recall anyone's refusing to eat what was served. The old adage said it all: "Where He leads me, I will follow. What He feeds me, I will swallow."

Once when a friend invited us to dinner, the girls overheard the hostess say, "I always like cooking for the Jones girls. They eat what you make." With that, she served oysters, a delicacy our girls didn't appreciate. They still remember the difficulty they had in swallowing the oysters.

With their Welsh heritage from David, it was only natural the girls enjoyed singing. They made up a tape of choruses, and we gave away more than 200 copies to folks who wanted them. As a trio, they sang for weddings, services, and other special occasions. They always sang for kindergarten commencement. One little fellow was describing the activities to his mother: "Then all the Miss Joneses in the whole school will sing!"

Even though we loved having the girls with us, I felt a growing concern for them. One day, when I was working in the kitchen and David was on the back porch with his Bible, I said to him through the screen door, "This isn't right. The girls are a blessing to us, but they need to be starting their own homes. The Lord doesn't seem to have husbands for them here."

After a bit, David came in with an encouraging word: "The Lord told me He has plans for the girls and things in store for them that beat anything you can imagine now. *'Rejoice and give thanks for My thoughts and plans for them,'* He said."

David was right. We never could have imagined all that the Lord had in mind for them.

As I brought in the mail on June 23, 1973, my eyes lit up.

"Look at this!" I said, handing a brochure to David. The First World Conference on the Holy Spirit was to be held in Jerusalem from February 28 to March 3 of 1974. "No trip to Israel has ever seemed just right for us, but this one does. Oh, how I'd love to go!"

The list of speakers was a roster of "who's who" in charismatic circles: Corrie ten Boom, Kathryn Kuhlman, Pat Robertson, Art Katz, and others. Four thousand were expected to attend.

"Let's pray about it," David said as he laid hands on the brochure. "Lord, if this is the time for us to see Your land, please make it possible."

For more than two years, we had not had a guaranteed dollar. Whatever folks felt led to share of their own volition was our income. We were in a position where only a miracle could provide the funds for such a trip.

Two days later a dear friend, Jewell Masten, handed us a check for $1,000 with these words: "I wish you'd use it to go to Israel." We were overwhelmed! I had brought the brochure in my purse, thinking she and Henry might be interested.

"Why yes, that looks like the ideal trip for us. I believe we'll go," she responded enthusiastically.

The Holy Land! Thrilling, exciting! Obviously the Lord was in it and would provide the rest of the money needed for the trip.

David signed up as a tour leader and began adding to our party. After we had enough people to make my trip free, we realized we'd probably have another free trip to give away. We had two friends we felt the Lord would have us invite. One had recently gone through a traumatic divorce; the other was a widow. The first had to decline the invitation because her daughter was getting married, and the second had an equally valid reason not to accept the offer.

Then David and I remembered a statement made by a woman who had taken a group of young people to the Holy Land: "The best investment you can make for a young person spiritually is to take them to Israel." Could it be the Lord wanted our teenager, Ann, to have such an experience? She was ecstatic over the prospect.

We kept adding to our group till we had eighteen, including my beloved Aunt Verona from New Bern, North Carolina. Such a large group entitled us to three-and-a-half free trips, so we invited all three girls. Barbara and Gwen hesitantly asked their principal for permission.

"Indeed. Any teacher will be more valuable for such an experience," was the wise man's reply.

So it was that our entire family took off on this life-changing trip.

I have claimed that Israel is to other lands what the Bible is to other books--but I was unprepared for the emotional impact as El Al landed at Lod Airport in Tel Aviv. The four-hundred Christians aboard laughed, cried, and clapped as we touched ground.

Heavenly excitement filled Jerusalem, if not all Israel, as four-thousand charismatic Christians gathered. Israel's economy had suffered from the 1973 Yom Kippur war. Now all businesses had a new burst of life with the blessing of our joyful presence.

A group of happy Germans shared our floor at the Pilgrim Palace, a small Arab hotel opposite the Damascus gate, almost in the shadow of Gordon's Calvary. It was thrilling to go out on our balcony at night and enjoy the lights on the wall that surrounds the Old City. It was all any of us had dreamed--and more.

"Will all of you who have heard Kathryn Kuhlman before please give your seats that others may hear?" came over the loudspeaker as we gathered for a healing service. The bulging walls couldn't hold all those who had come. Many of us happily went elsewhere and saw the service on a television screen. We didn't know it at the time, but her ministry was soon to end.

There were many testimonies as amazing as ours as to how the Lord had provided for the trip. One young mother of three, in limited circumstances, seemed to walk on air, hardly daring to believe the Lord had provided for her to come. For our entire family to enjoy such a spiritual feast was a miracle.

On the afternoon Art Katz spoke, David and I, along with the Mastens, Paul Reinke, Aunt Verona, and Lala Day, took a taxi to deliver a gift to the Leper

Home in Ramallah--so we missed his talk. Later we learned he had asked all who wanted to serve God's chosen people, the Jews, to stand. Both Barbara and Gwen, who had read and loved *Appointment in Jerusalem*, the story of Derek Prince's first wife, Lydia, stood to their feet and made a commitment they meant from their hearts.

That commitment began the outworking of God's plans for our girls--the plans that "beat anything we could imagine."

Ever since I had been saved in 1957, I had pondered Peter's command to "repent, and be baptized every one of you in the name of Jesus Christ" (Acts 2:38).

My baptism by sprinkling when I was a baby had not followed any repentance on my part. Nor had my confirmation at the age of eleven been preceded by heart searching and remorse for sin. Should I seek another baptism? One day, many years before our trip to Israel, I put out a fleece: "Lord, if You want me to be baptized by immersion, let me get to the Jordan River." At the time, that seemed as improbable for me as walking on the moon.

Our last day in Israel was to include a boat trip on the Sea of Galilee and a bus stop by the Jordan River for baptisms. Through the influence of Baptist friends, Barbara and Gwen had already been immersed. Now David, Ann, and I planned to take advantage of this God-provided opportunity. By the end of our tour, however, several inches of snow had fallen, and I had a nasty head cold.

The night before our scheduled baptisms, I slept fitfully. It seemed as though the devil was in the room, taunting me: "You'll lose the hearing in your good ear if you go in that freezing water." (As a teenager, I had lost all hearing in one ear following a case of mumps.)

Finally, at dawn, I met Satan head on: "Devil, I don't care what you say, I am going to be baptized in the Jordan today."

Our friend Paul Reinke and a black brother baptized David, who in turn baptized Ann and me, as well as a Methodist pastor and his wife, Homer and Evelyn Martin. As Ann and I stepped into the river, the water was frigid.

"I'll never make it!" I said to Ann. Then a miracle happened: I was not conscious of any more discomfort. We were immersed, and it was as though Jesus took the cold out of the water. Once again, He had done above all I could ask or think.

18--A Real Smorgasbord

All vestiges of snacks had been wiped away and lap trays replaced as the plane glided to a stop at the Stockholm airport.

Our group, representing various chapters of the FGBMFI (Full Gospel Businessmen's Fellowship International), had assembled in Boston in the spring of 1976. Wanting a vacation with a spiritual purpose, and receiving a gift to finance it, David and I had joined several dozen other Spirit-baptized Christians for the Scandinavian Airlift. For two weeks, the group would fan out over European countries with the object of sharing our Christian testimonies. David and I were assigned to Sweden.

Even though it was late April, snow-covered ground greeted us in Stockholm. Our four-day stay at the Birger Jarl Hotel (owned and operated by the State church) was filled with sightseeing by day and attending services in various churches in the evenings.

"Where can we get a genuine Scandinavian smorgasbord?" we asked Brother Carlson, our leader.

"Forget it. Prices are sky-high. Find a McDonald's and save the smorgasbord for back home. It's more reasonable there." He was right. Nothing was cheap.

As we brought our packed bags to the lobby on the morning of the fifth day, excitement rippled through the crowd. After receiving our assignments, we would spread over Sweden in small groups, staying in private homes for a week. The six in our group headed for the train station.

A two-hour ride due west brought us to Orebro, where our hostess, Gerda Gunnarson, met us. She and her husband, Arne, had a comfortable home in the country. Half our group stayed with Arne's brother's family, across the road.

How we enjoyed the Swedish meals, fun, and fellowship! It was amazing to discover that the Christians in Sweden were being taught the same truths we were.

Gerda didn't care for the teaching that the man is head of the house.

"Well," she concluded, "if Arne's the head, then I'm the neck that turns the head." The way she handled her job at a hatchery, meals (with the help of her daughter), and taking us to minister in schools, jail, and churches proved her point.

After five packed days, no further opportunities for ministry could be found for our last two days in Orebro, so David and I decided to give our hosts a break and leave early. We wanted to go to Holland, to see the tulip gardens and "the hiding place," from which Corrie ten Boom's book took its name. Then we planned to rejoin the group in Brussels.

Upon arriving back in Stockholm, we dragged our cumbersome luggage from train to bus to airport. Happily, we presented our tickets at the window.

"You can't do this," the agent said as he studied our credentials. "These tickets must be used with the group."

Going separately would cost an additional $400 in American money, he told us.

Tired, hungry, and discouraged, I remembered reading in a travel brochure about an inexpensive mini-cruise from Stockholm to Helsinki. With only two free days, it was a long chance but worth a try.

Yellow pages in Sweden are, unfortunately, printed in Swedish, which is "Greek" to me. Two numbers that looked like travel agencies brought forth only Swedish voices and no satisfaction.

"Perhaps Annica can help us," I suggested to David. (Annica had been an exchange student to the United States, and we had visited in her home.) She answered the phone when I called, but said she was busy feeding her toddlers. She promised to call back in twenty minutes,

With flagging hopes, I returned to David. To my surprise, the defeated husband I had left a few minutes earlier was all excited.

"Someone over in Helsinki needs us!" he told me. "I just opened my Bible and was reading about Paul's call to Macedonia. The Spirit quickened it to me. We are to go to Helsinki to minister." He was suddenly refreshed and enthusiastic.

"Don't be silly." It was my turn to be negative. "First, it would take a miracle of timing for it to work--not to mention reservations, funds, and all that. Second, we don't speak the language. How could we possibly minister?"

In exactly twenty minutes, the phone rang. Now Annica was excited. "Would you believe it? I got you the last two reservations on the ship! Report to the dock. You will sail at 6:00 P.M. and arrive at Helsinki after breakfast. You will return Tuesday night."

It was perfect timing, and the price was right. David was jubilant. Didn't this prove the Lord was in it?

I was just eager for the cruise.

As the ship slipped quietly away from Stockholm, we enjoyed watching the Swedish archipelago with its inviting-looking houses on the smallest of islands. We dressed in our tiny cabin for a late dinner and were thrilled to find a sumptuous Swedish smorgasbord. Just what we had asked for in Sweden! Lulled by the waves, we slept like babes that night.

Breakfast, abundant in eggs and cheeses, was served early. Immediately after the meal, we disembarked and promptly piled onto a tour bus.

Our guide spoke several languages. Since we were the only English-speaking passengers, he only occasionally got around to telling us about the sights. He did mention a small shopping center called "The Forum" and Stockman's Department Store.

"Let's start with Stockman's," I suggested as we left the tour. The store had a huge window display in red, white and blue, to honor our Bicentennial. For us, it was a touching sight so far from home.

"Don't you remember? Finland was the only country to repay us their debt after World War I," David, the history buff, reminded me.

We tried asking questions of clerks in the store, people at the information booth, and several intelligent-looking shoppers, but nobody spoke English. Finally a customer, an Englishwoman in a tweed suit, overheard me asking where the ladies' room was. She directed me. Then I had to deal with an attendant who expected a fee--in Finnish coins, of course.

When we left the store, it seemed to me that everyone in Helsinki was out for lunch. All walked briskly, whether for lunch or exercise we couldn't tell. There must have been five abreast on the wide sidewalk.

Then David did a very uncharacteristic thing. Never before had he ever suggested shopping--but in a good clear voice addressed to me he said, "I wonder where the Forum is."

With that, a tall young man on crutches swung around. "You're headed in the wrong direction," he said. "Follow me. I will take you to it."

We could hardly believe the split-second timing: that this English-speaking Finn should approach us at the precise moment of David's inquiry.

Together we walked and talked. Carl, twenty-eight, told us he worked for Pan Am, had been to the States several times, and was on sick leave because of a broken ankle. He lived with his mother.

His father had died recently, but that wasn't his only heartache. "I had a younger brother serving with our navy. While his ship was docked in Israel, he sent us a card in which he spoke of having had some kind of religious experience. Then he died, most unexpectedly. I have been wondering so much what kind of experience he had."

Such an incredible answer to prayer! Our assignment was clear. By now, we had reached The Forum. Benches were designed for two. Excusing myself to shop, I left, silently praying and praising the Lord. I knew David would be explaining to Carl that we are all born in sin and only the blood of Jesus can obtain our pardon. By asking forgiveness and inviting Jesus into our hearts, we can have the slate wiped clean and be assured of a home in heaven.

Two smiling faces greeted my return. "Carl's name has just been written in the Lamb's Book of Life," David announced triumphantly. From the joy on Carl's face, it was obvious he now understood his brother's experience. What a bonus to know he would see him again!

Swinging along on his crutches, Carl walked with us several miles to the ship, the three of us talking all the way. Carl was soaking up Bible truths like a blotter. He couldn't learn fast enough. He had a Bible at home, he said. I dug out of my suitcase a copy of *From Prison to Praise* by Merlin Carothers and gave it to him. It carried the message Carl needed: out of all trials the Lord can bring a blessing if we thank Him for the circumstances.

Departure was nearing. We had good prayer with Carl and said goodbye. Then we stood at the rail and waved to him as long as visibility allowed.

That evening, we enjoyed our second smorgasbord with overflowing hearts, as we thought how magnificently the Lord had answered our prayer to be used of Him.

Once settled in the Sheraton Hotel in Brussels, we left the group for an afternoon in order to make our trip to Holland. The train to Haarlem took us through the Dutch countryside of windmills and fields of tulips. From Haarlem, a bus took us to the beautiful Kukenoff Gardens, where the tulips were in their last week of blooming.

Next, we looked up the ten Boom home and watch shop. We had read *The Hiding Place* and seen the movie so often we could have conducted the tour. David crawled through the wall opening into "the hiding place"--the tiny crawl space to which the Jews who were being sheltered by the ten Booms had fled that fateful night in 1944. Most of the ten Boom family died in Nazi prison camps for giving shelter to God's chosen people. How fortunate for the world that Corrie survived to tell their story!

On our last evening in Brussels, a banquet was held with representatives from the English, Scandinavian, and European chapters of the FGBMFI, along with our own delegation. The speaker was Fred Ladenius, a man of God who entertained us royally with a humorous but inspiring message. Our laughter brought out the help. Sitting near the back, we saw an opportunity for ministry.

We left our seats and approached a waiter. David, with the little French he had absorbed in World War II, and with a Bible in hand, went to work. He pointed heavenward, then to his heart, then to the Word. Did the gentleman want to give his heart to Jesus?

"*Oui.*" He seemed eager. We bowed our heads, and David put his hand on the young man's shoulder and prayed the sinner's prayer for him. Then he went to the book table and bought a New Testament in French as a gift for his new convert. We repeated the process for two more waiters and a timid cleaning maid, cloth in hand. Then the headwaiter appeared and angrily ordered them back whence they had come, thus ending our missionary endeavors.

David gave Carl's name and address to the president of the Helsinki chapter of the FGBMFI, who promised to get in touch with him and invite him to their fellowship.

When our plane landed at the Greensboro, North Carolina, airport, we were delighted to see our daughters. They too had a lot to report. Ann had been named yearbook editor for her upcoming senior year at Edgewood Christian School. Barbara and Gwen told us of their meeting with Wilbur and Betty Presson from Israel, who had invited them to serve in a Christian youth hostel in Haifa.

That summer, Gwen resigned her teaching position to serve as a volunteer in the hostel. Barbara followed the next year. The hostel was an ideal vehicle to attract young people. Friday-evening services held there were frequented by sailors stationed at the Haifa port. Very likely, Carl's brother had attended one of these services and received Christ as his Savior there. It is a small world indeed.

After eighteen months in Haifa, Gwen returned to the States and married Rick Hanger, whom she had met in the hostel. Rick had just finished a four-year stint with the Navy in Italy, and had gone to Israel to spend a year in study at Hebrew University. When he visited Haifa, what better place to stay than in a Christian hostel? Rick is now a Presbyterian minister.

Barbara spent four years at the hostel, then taught at the Anglican School in Jerusalem for four more years. Since her marriage, she and her husband have continued to live in Jerusalem.

An interesting note about the girls' marriages: Since the Lord had answered my prayer and chosen my husband for me years ago, I had wanted His choice for the girls. "Lord, let the sign be that You will speak to the young men and tell each one that our daughter is the wife You've chosen for him. There is no need to speak to the girls or to us, but please make it so clear to the men that they can never doubt You were in it."

He did just that. Each of our three sons-in-law remembers the details of where and when the Lord told him, *"This woman is to be your wife."*

At each of the weddings, David gave the invitation for salvation. All three couples were in complete agreement that each person present should have an opportunity to accept Christ as Savior. Four of the wedding guests later told us they had prayed the sinner's prayer after hearing David's invitation.

19--Gates of Glory

"If you want to see Dad again, you had better come now." The call from David's sister Dorothy, in January of 1977, sent us packing our suitcases, bundling up, and heading north in one of the worst winters in years. David's mother had gone to be with the Lord nine years earlier, after more than fifty years of praying for his dad's salvation. Ever since David and I had found the Lord, we too had had a burden to see Dad saved. We had to try one more time.

Barbara and Ann went with us. Fortunately, the roads were clear, and we drove right to St. Elizabeth's Hospital in Youngstown, Ohio.

"How are you doing, Trite?" David asked his dad, using the old nickname they had for each other.

"Pretty good, son," belied the obvious weakness he was feeling.

We stayed with Dorothy and her husband, Burt, for three days. I took over the meals while David and his two sisters, Dorothy Honey and Florence Daggett, took turns sitting with Dad. David would read Scripture to him and pray for him, but there was no breakthrough. A lifelong habit of avoiding anything of a spiritual nature was hard to break. When Dad had been well enough, he would leave the room to avoid any such discussions. Now he was a captive audience.

On the morning we were to return home, a new snowstorm was brewing. With a 450-mile trip ahead, our farewell visit to Dad had to be short. The girls and I went along to Dad's room, visited briefly, and kissed him goodbye. David wanted one more chance to visit with him alone.

"Girls," I suggested, "let's go for a cup of coffee and have prayer." We made our way to the basement cafeteria of St. Elizabeth's. The nonsmoking area in the rear was fortunately empty. There was nothing to prevent a good, fervent prayer session. Barbara, Ann, and I bowed our heads. We enthusiastically agreed that in these final moments, the Holy Spirit would do His mighty work and make Grandpa receptive. I heard myself adding, "And Lord, please make it so clear that David will never have to wonder if Dad really asked You into his heart." Yet as we returned to the lobby, I confess to doubting such a miracle could happen.

Snow was driving down at a rate that boded no good for traveling that day. Somewhat anxiously, we waited for David.

When the elevator door opened, he came out beaming. From ear to ear there was nothing but a grin. With a look outside, we decided to get started immediately. Time enough for the good news later.

For the first 130 miles, we drove on solid ice, with snow pelting down furiously. Amazingly, we never slipped or slid, but maintained a steady pace. In the opposite lane, a tractor-trailer had jackknifed and cars were backed up half a mile. But our lane stayed clear.

As the miles slipped by, David told his tale. "I was reading to Dad in Romans 8. As I got to the ninth verse--'Now if any man have not the Spirit of Christ, he is none of his'--Dad stopped me. Never in my seventeen years in the ministry had he asked me a spiritual question. But he said, 'What does that mean, Trite?'

"I explained the verse, then asked, 'Dad, would you like to be one of His? May I lead you in a prayer asking Jesus to come into your heart and forgive your sins?'

"Without hesitation, he clearly answered yes."

David led him in the sinner's prayer, and Dad prayed after him. The matter was forever settled.

Three days later, Dad sank into a coma. Three weeks later, just before his ninety-third birthday, he slipped away--into the arms of Jesus.

We thought things had been tight financially when Barbara went to Wheaton and her college costs amounted to more than two-thirds of David's yearly salary. But when Ann was ready to go, sixteen years later, college costs had more than doubled. And this time we had no salary, parsonage, hospitalization, or material benefits of any kind. Still, we believed God's best for Ann was a Christian school. She applied at Oral Roberts University and was accepted.

Periodically, I expected the Lord to release me to work again, but He never did. Real estate had always attracted me. The home we were renting in Winston-Salem was to be sold to make room for a highway. It was a temptation to buy it, have it moved, and resell it. A lovely wooded lot nearby was available at an excellent price. By sealed bid, the house was mine for a ridiculously low figure. However, the Lord permitted a technical error that awarded the house to another bidder. As He closed that door of opportunity, I finally accepted the fact that nothing in my life was to take precedence over David's calling.

When it was time for Ann to enter ORU in 1977, David and I decided to take her to Tulsa and let that trip be our vacation. As we headed back home after getting our daughter settled, I said happily to David, "My, I can't wait to see what the Lord has in mind for dinner tonight." That morning, we had asked the Lord to order our day.

Eating out was always a treat. To be truthful, I should have admitted that my system was bogged down by days of eating fried fish, hush puppies, french fries, and other hard-to-digest foods. Still, I wanted to make the most of every meal during our three-day, leisurely drive home.

"Isn't it marvelous," I continued, "that when you commit your way to the Lord He does things just right?"

Together, David and I reviewed Ann's college set-up. We recalled with gratitude the elderly parking-lot attendant who had blessed us as we arrived, the lovely campus, her dorm room, her roommate, and the satisfying lunch we had enjoyed in the dining hall before saying goodbye.

"Oh, honey!" I exclaimed suddenly. "We missed our turn-off back there. I'm sorry, I just wasn't paying attention." Since I'm the navigator when we travel, the error was mine. "But never mind: the Lord must have something better up ahead."

This area of the Midwest was new to us. The interstate stretched in one long thread. I little knew the long, deserted areas between cities.

The next exit showed nothing, but the following one had a sign proclaiming gas and food were available. With relief and eager anticipation of a lovely restaurant awaiting us, we veered to the right and headed into the woods. Both of us were weary from our long ride, and we had more miles to go before we would reach the motel where we had a reservation for the night.

Two buildings greeted us. A dilapidated gas station on the left was obviously no longer in business. The other, on the right, was a combination gas station and restaurant; there wasn't a car in sight. Trying the door, we found it open. Happily, we sank down at a table, hoping for the best.

A young boy about twelve brought a menu. "How about the fried-chicken platter?" I asked confidently.

Before David could give his order, the youngster disappeared. After a trip to the kitchen, he returned to announce, "We don't have chicken."

"All right," I answered agreeably. "How about the beef dinner?"

Another check. "We don't have that either," he said.

"Maybe we'd better begin again. What do you have?"

"Well, ma'am, we close soon and all we could serve would be soup we have in cans. Tomato?" he suggested hopefully.

"All right," I answered. David said he'd take tomato soup too. And coffee.

Our youthful waiter soon returned with a coffeepot, but there was only one cup of coffee left in it. We split it.

As we adjusted to the unexpected, we realized the cook (we had learned she was the boy's mother) could be seen from the table, and we could visit with her as she opened the can and heated the soup.

Noting a small TV in the kitchen, we remarked it must be a welcome diversion for one who was so alone.

"Yes," she agreed. "I work long hours. Then when I go home, I have a husband and four boys to take care of. I don't like these long hours, seven days a week. I'm a Christian, and I don't like not getting to church anymore. I don't know how much longer I can keep it up."

We asked if she ever saw "The 700 Club."

"Oh yes!" she returned. "I don't know what I'd do without it."

Our hearts went out to this valiant little mother, trying desperately to hold down her job and keep things going at home. Obviously she was discouraged and near a breaking point.

When we finished our soup and coffee, it was time for us to leave and for her to close up shop. We asked if she would like for us to have prayer together. Her son joined us, and the four of us formed a little circle, held hands, and prayed. We asked the Lord to free her for another job or cut out the Sunday work; to give her strength at work and at home; and to bless the family. When we finished, she seemed refreshed. Her husband arrived to take them home, and we left.

As we drove down the road, I summed up the situation: "That wasn't the meal I had in mind, but I must admit I feel good on that soup. And being used of the Lord to encourage one of His saints is more satisfying than food. He did guide us to just the right place after all."

As for Ann and ORU, she loved all four years there, even though she had to work to help pay her tuition and board. When she married a classmate, Gary Gillman, in the summer after their graduation in 1981, her roommate, Laura Braugh, and two other college friends--Maggie Radd and Rhonda Hellstern--flew to Virginia Beach for the wedding. Dear friends for a lifetime. Our cup was running over.

20--"'700 Club'--may I help you?"

In 1978, we received an invitation from Gwen's mother-in-law, Gretchen: "Can't you come and spend Thanksgiving here in Virginia Beach?" David and I were alone that fall, and were delighted to go.

Besides having a good visit and getting better acquainted with Gretchen, we had an opportunity to visit Pat Robertson's morning TV program, "The 700 Club," where Gretchen was hostess. It just happened that a new set was being made, and there would be no live show until later in the day. The visitors who came that Friday morning were going to be disappointed.

After Gretchen had given her talk and taken the group on a brief tour of CBN headquarters, we sat in the chapel waiting for the set to be finished. I nudged David. "This reminds me of our meetings," I said. "Why not offer to minister to any needs folks have? We've all got time on our hands." So David got up and told them his credentials for ministering.

What a time! One woman had terrible eczema and hadn't been able to put her hands in water for years. Her poor husband did all the dishes and housework after he got home from work. This was their vacation trip, and they had driven far to get there, hoping for help. Not only did we have good prayer for her, but her husband accepted Jesus! That made her as happy as the healing we trust she received for her skin.

A man had chest pains that left after prayer. Another man had one leg shorter than the other, a condition that was corrected as we prayed. About ten of the visitors had ministry before the set was ready and the program started.

That night, we were sitting by Gretchen's desk as she worked on her church newsletter. She casually remarked, "Marshall and I held hands and agreed that, when the new center opens next year, David Jones will be the minister to guests. They need one." (Marshall was a Wake Forest graduate who had attended some of our meetings before coming to CBN University as a student.)

We talked this over on the way home and decided that David should apply for the position. When we returned to Virginia Beach in the spring, to bring Ann and her roommate to visit CBN, Gretchen made two appointments for interviews. Neither offered any encouragement. There was a freeze on hiring. Since we hadn't been eager to leave Winston-Salem, it didn't matter one way or the other.

A few months later, on a lovely late-summer morning, I held a toddler's hand as we circled our house during Tuesday morning prayer meeting. "Lord, don't You think I've had enough nursery duty?" I complained. "After all, I've taken my stint over the years. Now here I am, at fifty-nine, still having to take out all restless or crying babies and toddlers so service isn't disrupted. I'm really tired of it."

Then a realization of the Lord's great goodness to us hit me. "Oh, Lord, I apologize! When I gave my life to You years ago, there were no strings attached. Even though I would rather be doing soul-winning, if You want me on nursery detail, I'll not complain again. With Your help, I'll do it cheerfully."

I believe I passed a test.

The next Tuesday morning--September 11, 1979-- after the coffee was made and Harry and Flo Martin had arrived with the doughnuts, the phone rang. The call was for David.

"This is Tommy Coy, Director of Spiritual Life at CBN. Pat has just approved the hiring of a minister, and you are our choice. Could you possibly come next week and be acclimated before the official opening of the new center?"

"I'm sure we can," David said, as only a man would. That gave us one week to hold all regular meetings, say goodbye, locate a house, and *move!*

Early the next morning, I flew out to spend the day house-hunting in Virginia Beach. The Lord prepared the way, and Gretchen had done her homework. The town house we rented, and later bought, proved to be ideal for our needs and taste.

Virtie Stroup, religious writer for the *Winston-Salem Journal*, gave David over half a page of pictures and story about our meetings and future plans. She included a grand write-up on the new CBN Center. This final story was in keeping with all her news coverage of David and his stand. It was always fairly presented, with never an error, to my knowledge.

We got in a last session with all seven of our groups. On Sunday afternoon, Lorene Porter and Zola Tiller held a farewell reception at the Porter home. Such a dear thing to do, on such short notice! It blessed us to say goodbye to two-hundred or so dear friends.

Since the van was engaged to come Tuesday and we had Sunday services on schedule, no packing was done ahead of time. When Rose Hill announced she was taking a day off from her job to get us packed, I heaved a great sigh of relief. Harry and Flo Martin, Mary Everhart, Nancy Dobbins, Naomi Venable, and others appeared at eight o'clock Monday morning. Jonnie Crosman used her station wagon to haul cartons all morning. How they worked! They didn't find my pack-rat ways a help; but dear David, as always, stoutly defended the blessing my thrifty management had been as he sought the Lord above money. By 1:30, all was neatly packaged and waiting on the porch and in the carport for the moving van.

The work finished, we were free to visit with all who came. With all those boxes outside, we couldn't leave the house, and we were beginning to wonder what we would do about eating. Just then, Ray and Anne Wenger drove up with the best packed lunch! It lasted for days. All was so wholesome, snacks included.

The entire trip to Virginia Beach--in two cars--went smoothly, and we were waiting at our town house when the van arrived at eight o'clock Wednesday morning.

The official dedication of the new CBN quarters on October 6 was televised for all to see. David's nine o'clock service for visitors each morning in the prayer chapel was the highlight of his day. Almost every day reflected the power and activity of the Holy Spirit in saving souls, healing bodies, and filling believers with the Holy Spirit. A brother in Christ, Dick Hudgins or Dick James, usually assisted David in the chapel service.

One day a young surgeon had a prayer request. "I'm on vacation," he said. "When I return, I must remove a brain tumor from a young boy. I would like the Lord to do it first." Everyone in the chapel joined in earnest prayer.

A few weeks later, the doctor called CBN and asked for David. "I have wonderful news!" he exclaimed. "We did another x-ray of the boy's head, and the tumor is gone. Praise the Lord!"

After the chapel service, David spent the rest of his day in counseling and phone ministry. Among the many whom he counseled were two women struggling with fears. One, on her trip to CBN, was too fearful to drive the seventeen-mile bridge and tunnel that spanned the Chesapeake Bay. One of the tunnel employees had to take the wheel for her. After being born again and receiving the baptism in the Holy Spirit, she was able to drive herself through the tunnel on the way home, praying in her prayer language the entire way.

The other woman was already saved and Spirit-filled and could not understand her continual fears. David asked, "Did you suffer a dreadful scare as a child?" After a momentary pause, David came out with a question that just *had* to be inspired by the Holy Spirit, because he had no natural way of knowing anything in the woman's childhood:

"Could you have been thrown into the water to learn to swim?" he asked. It was clearly a word of knowledge, one of the gifts of the Holy Spirit (see I Corinthians 12:8).

Her jaw dropped. "How did you know? That's exactly what happened."

It was a small matter for him to dismiss the spirit of fear in the name of Jesus.

For myself, I couldn't believe what the Lord had done. I was a volunteer counselor on the phones two mornings a week, as well as during telethons or whenever there was a need. The very thing I most wanted to do, soul-winning, was arranged perfectly by such a set-up. What blessings have taken place over those phone wires, only heaven knows.

From its infancy, "The 700 Club" provided counseling for its viewers. The idea was that Spirit-filled believers would agree with them in prayer according to Matthew 18:19:

> *"If two of you shall agree on earth as touching any thing that they shall ask, it shall be done for them of my Father which is in heaven."*

"'700 Club'--may I help you?" I asked on my usual stint of telephone volunteer work at CBN.

"I'm afraid not. I doubt that anybody can help me," a forlorn voice answered, sounding as if it were coming from down in a deep well. "Our marriage is about over. I'm sure my husband is going to leave me. I don't know what I'll do. I've never worked."

Poor man! I thought. *To come home from a hard day's work to such a dreary-sounding wife.*

"What seems to be the problem?" I began. The picture she gave was gloomy. He was having troubles at work and was uncommunicative when he arrived home. The marriage was one big zero--just nothing left.

"As a starter, are you a Christian? I don't mean being a member of a church. Was there a time when you saw yourself as a lost sinner and invited Jesus into your heart?"

"No, not really," she answered.

"Would you like to do that?" I continued.

"Yes." She seemed eager.

After giving her the Scriptures, "For all have sinned, and come short of the glory of God" (Romans 3:23) and "Believe on the Lord Jesus Christ, and thou shalt be saved" (Acts 16:31), I led her in the sinner's prayer.

Next I recommended she read *How to Be the Wife of a Happy Husband*, by Darien Cooper (Wheaton, IL: Victor Books), and suggested she try to find a Bible-study or prayer group for fellowship.

"It's a thrilling role the Lord has given us wives," I continued. "We have a responsibility to our husbands. We should make our home a place to which they are eager to return. . . .

"Why not surprise your husband tonight?" I added. "Until you can get that book, here are some suggestions. Clean up the house and dress most attractively by the time your husband comes home from work. Prepare one of his favorite meals. Meet him at the door. Ask about his day's work. Show an interest in each detail. That will show you how to be praying for him while he's at work."

Stopping for breath, I realized I had heard nothing from her.

"Is this making any sense?" I asked.

"Oh, lady!" She spoke slowly and clearly. "You've no idea how much sense it's making. Now what did you say was the name of that book?"

We closed with good prayer, asking the Lord's guidance as she sought to be a loving Christian wife and asking help for the husband at work even then, and for a blessing upon their home.

As I hung up the phone, I smiled. What would that husband think when he came home from work and found a totally different wife from the woman he had left that morning? Just making one phone call, praying to receive Jesus into her heart, and following suggestions from an older married woman had given the distressed woman a totally new outlook. No wonder such calls were among my favorites.

Another call was quite different. When I asked this woman if I could help her, the wires almost sparked.

"It's that husband of mine. That good-for-nothing punk went off to work and told me to pack his suitcase for a business trip this afternoon. There's nothing wrong with him that he can't pack his own bag."

As she stopped for breath and to collect more words to criticize her husband, I hastened to get in the driver's seat.

"Now help me get the picture," I interrupted. "You do not have to work outside the home--is that correct?"

"Yes," she admitted.

"And your husband is at work now and will take a flight this afternoon after work?"

"Yes," she answered. The contempt was diminishing.

"All right. I grant he may not have asked you in a pleasing manner, but it doesn't seem unreasonable to me that you should pack his things. Why not have fun at it? Write little notes and put them with his clothes. Messages like, 'Miss you,' 'Love you,' or 'Hurry home.' He'd like that."

We discussed her standing with the Lord. Then I suggested the book I always recommended to wives. She was responding beautifully. Suddenly she was inspired.

"You know what, lady? I must hang up. I think I'll get dressed and surprise him by going downtown and having lunch with him before he leaves."

I especially enjoyed receiving calls from singles. One young man called to report that his girl friend had broken off with him the evening before, after years of dating. He felt he couldn't go on. I learned he had never committed his heart and life to the Lord, and we soon remedied that.

"Now you are in an ideal situation," I told him. "Study the story in Genesis 24 of how Abraham's servant selected the wife for Isaac. He said, 'I being in the way, the Lord led me' [v. 27]. You can pray about your wife, put out a fleece, and let the Lord select her. If it's the girl you've been dating, He can speak to her. If not, you're free for whomever the Lord chooses." We had a good prayer together and he hung up with a totally different outlook.

One morning at 10:40, the dearest-sounding young woman called. "I'm a college student, not married, and I'm pregnant. My father's a minister, and it would just kill my folks if they knew, so I have an appointment for an abortion at one o'clock. I just had to talk to someone."

We had a blessed exchange. I told her that her sin was not unforgivable, but she shouldn't add murder to it. Childless couples were praying mightily for babies, and it would be best for her to talk the situation over with her folks. She agreed to cancel the abortion and call home that evening. We prayed together and asked the Lord to prepare her parents and give them wisdom.

That evening, David and I were much in prayer for them, and we trust a precious little life was spared.

Occasionally we would get an obscene call. Instructions were to hang up immediately. But as I started to put down the receiver on the worst blasphemy I had ever heard, the Spirit stopped me. *"Don't put that down. Keep him on the line. Keep talking."*

So while this man spewed forth filth, I kept repeating, "Jesus loves you. Jesus is the answer. Why not give your heart to Jesus?" Eventually he settled down, and I learned he was calling from Las Vegas, had found our number on a scrap of paper in an alley, and had telephoned out of curiosity. I kept insisting it would be good for him to pray and get forgiveness for his sins and invite Jesus into his heart. "Won't you pray this prayer with me?" I asked.

"Well, if it makes you happy," he finally agreed.

"Oh, sir, it would make me very happy," I said truthfully.

Much to my surprise, this filthy-mouthed man prayed the sinner's prayer after me as meek as a lamb. When we finished, and he went off into profanity again, I excused myself and hung up. I make no claim that he had a life-changing experience--but I do believe the Lord's hand is on him and a start was made.

"Despise not small beginnings," I reminded myself.

A retired couple who volunteered frequently at the phones told of an unusual day. The husband had a call from Chicago. A woman in a motel had been attacked and raped and was in a terrible condition. While on the phone, she gave her heart to Jesus and prayed the sinner's prayer. After getting her name, address, age, etc., our friend made her promise to call for help. When he and his wife were on their lunch break, he told her about the call.

They had barely returned to the phones when the wife had a call.

"I'm a paramedic here in Chicago, and I've been called to this motel. A woman is sitting by the phone, but she's dead. In her hand is a piece of paper with your number on it. Can you tell me anything about her?"

The wife said she'd get her husband, as he had talked with the woman. Out of dozens of phones at the CBN counseling center, the call came right to one of the two people who knew about the situation!

After the husband had given the medic the requested information, he asked, "Now if *you* were to die today, are you ready to meet Jesus?" Then he led the young man to accept Jesus as his Savior too.

A family wrote to thank "The 700 Club" for the salvation of their mother, who had just been buried. They were afraid she had never accepted the Lord--but after the funeral they found in the mail a letter for her from "The 700 Club," along with a booklet. The letter said, "Since you called in and accepted Jesus as your Lord and Savior, this is the material we promised to send."

Imagine those children's supreme joy when they realized that their mother, of her own volition, had called in for the express purpose of giving her heart to Jesus!

One Thursday morning I received requests to pray for many big needs: the healing of cancer, heart attacks, paralysis, mental retardation, etc. At a break between calls, I was telling the Lord that I was no Kathryn Kuhlman and didn't feel equal to all these huge prayer requests.

Just then Ben Kinchlow, who often co-hosted "The 700 Club" along with Pat Robertson, was giving praise reports on the television screen. A grandmother in West Virginia called to say her five-year-old grandson, for whom she had asked prayer, had been taken to the hospital for surgery--but before the operation another check was made and he was found to be healed, without the surgery. He was discharged, and she was thanking the Lord. I realized that had been one of my Monday calls. The Lord had kept my phone from ringing long enough for me to hear the good news. I gave thanks and went on praying with every caller, confident the Lord was hearing from heaven.

We were continually amazed at how the Lord matched up the caller with the best counselor for the particular problem. A young blind man applied to become a counselor, saying he thought that was one way he could serve the Lord. The head of counselors trained him, then sat in on his first call to see how it went.

Imagine his amazement when the very first call was from a lady extremely upset. Her son had been in an accident, and they had just been told he would be blind. The new counselor was uniquely equipped to comfort her.

Once a young mother called practically in tears. She had quite a story.

"We're new in this community. I'm a nurse, and our children are in a day-care center. We're Christians, and my husband is the ideal father. He plays games with the children on the floor and gives them wholesome attention. Apparently our little four-year-old made a statement that some overly zealous social worker took to mean her father is molesting her. Nothing could be further from the truth, but you wouldn't believe how we're being harassed. Social Service workers have come to the house several times. They separate us from the children and quiz them relentlessly. We have no roots in the community and don't know where to turn." She named the town in the South.

"Would you believe this?" I asked her. "We just happen to have very dear Christian friends in your community! After we pray, I'll give you their names. They are community leaders, and I'm sure they could take care of this for you."

Later, on a trip south, we visited our friends in that town. They had indeed intervened. The family had joined their church and were a wonderful addition. Once again, the Lord had directed the call.

The first Christmas none of our daughters would be home, it seemed logical for us to spend Christmas Eve on the phones.

"There will be many lonely people out there, and most of the usual volunteers for that evening will want to be with their families," I told my husband. He agreed, and off we went.

As I stepped out of the car, an inner voice I had learned to recognize as the Lord spoke very clearly. *"Tell the first person who calls that I love him very much."*

As we walked arm in arm across the parking lot, I told David about the Lord's instructions.

When we arrived at the Center, they were indeed short of help. Those who had come were all busy on the phones. I settled quickly, had a brief prayer, and put the receiver on the hook. It rang immediately.

"'700 Club'--may I help you?" I answered.

"I doubt it," a man's belligerent voice replied.

"What seems to be the problem?" I asked.

"I'm sitting here with a gun in my hand. It's Christmas Eve. I not only didn't receive a gift, I didn't so much as get a card. I don't mean anything to anybody. I have *had* it."

Suddenly I remembered.

"Oh, sir! Have I got good news for you!"

"Wha--what?" He sounded excited.

"Well, as I got out of the car to come here, the Lord spoke to me and told me to tell the first person who called that He loved him very much. You are my first caller."

"Did He really?" he asked, incredulous.

"Indeed. Furthermore, He has never told me anything like that before. This proves He really cares about you, and His assurance of that love is the greatest Christmas gift of all.

"Since He has given you such a gift," I continued, "wouldn't you like to give Him the gift He most wants from you--your heart? He's gone to prepare a home for those who are His. All we have to do is repent of our sins and invite Him into our hearts, and He will accept us. Wouldn't you like to do that?"

156   *Peggy Jones*

"Oh my, yes!" he answered emphatically.

"Then just pray this prayer after me," I suggested. "Lord Jesus, please forgive me my sins, and come into my heart . . . and make me Yours. Thank you for doing it. In Jesus' Name."

He prayed after me so heartily I almost wept. As we finished, we were both overjoyed. I confirmed again what that step meant, urged him to join a Bible-believing church, and get into the Word--all of which he seemed eager to do.

Finally, I told him I had to get on to other calls. We were both sorry to hang up. I promised we'd meet in heaven and wished him the very best Christmas ever. I was in the midst of having a wonderful one myself.

Telethons involved hundreds of phones in three different studios. All hands were on deck: employees, spouses, volunteers, CBN (now Regent) University students and staff, and local congregations. Even young people helped out.

One boy, considered too young to handle calls, was a runner. That meant he would take our filled-out forms to the main studio, where the program was being aired. As he left the room, a phone was ringing. Someone had neglected to take the receiver off the hook. He felt sorry for the caller, so he answered.

"'700 Club'--may I help you?"

"Yes," a woman said. "I want to get saved."

After leading her in the sinner's prayer, he asked for her name and address, so material could be sent to her.

He started writing, then screamed, "Grandma!"

It was his own grandmother, for whose salvation he had been praying.

Only the Lord knows how many wondrous answers to prayer have come through the telephone ministry of "The 700 Club." I consider it one of the greatest privileges of my life to have had such a golden opportunity to work there. In everyday life, one rarely meets individuals hungry and thirsty for Jesus; yet every day at CBN folks called who were open to salvation, and often eager for it.

My fondest dreams of soul-winning were realized in that six-year period. I especially enjoyed opening up the vistas of salvation and the baptism in the Holy Spirit to nominal church members who had never known there was more--so much more!

Opportunities to minister were wonderful, but it wasn't all smooth sailing from the beginning. In our early days at CBN, I had a major hurdle to overcome.

Having slid my overnighter into the back seat of Nan's car, I fastened my seat belt and relaxed. As we left the Charleston, West Virginia, airport and began descending the hill, I knew I would have to talk fast. These few moments together, when she would meet my plane and take me to visit Mother, always went too quickly.

"Well, Nan," I began, "you are about to be able to check out the Bible. If it can be trusted, the Jones family will survive. If not, we'll starve to death." That was all I felt free to say, but I had to vent my feelings to someone. Who better than my sister in Christ, Nan Adams?

The long and the short of the current saga of the Jones's spiritual journey was that we had just given our savings away. For a thrifty German-Swiss descendant, this had been a real test.

It began six months earlier, when we left North Carolina and moved to Virginia Beach to work at the

Christian Broadcasting Network. As the family treasurer, I gave a report at dinner soon after settling in.

"Well, today I opened our account at the bank in the shopping center. I took the expired CD from Winston-Salem, plus other savings, and put it into one large CD here. It will mature in six months." I felt good about my report.

"I've been thinking," David began ominously. "When the CD matures, if you are in agreement, I would like to give it as a gift to CBN. It is almost beyond comprehension that such a place exists. Just think of it--people calling in day and night for salvation and needs of all kinds. Pat has the best all-around program. His benevolence-giving is wise. A gift to CBN is the best possible use of our money."

"You mean," I asked in unbelief, "you want to *give* our savings away?"

"I prefer to call it investing," was David's calm answer. "Imagine--if our gift could be used to bring folks to salvation. If just one person made it to heaven instead of hell, it would be worth it all."

"But our savings. . . . You want to give them away?" I was stunned.

"You have six months to pray about it. If it doesn't bear witness to your spirit, we'll not do it." With that, he closed the subject.

Pray I did. No answer came. Month after month slipped by. Surely the Lord would give a red or green light. When the six months were up, there had been no sign at all. As I transferred the money into our checking account, I realized a decision had to be made.

I remembered that the Lord often tested His people. Abraham took Isaac on a three-day journey, thinking he had to sacrifice him on Mount Moriah (see Genesis 22:1-13). When the rich young ruler came to

Jesus and was told he must give up his wealth, he went away sorrowful (see Matthew 19:21,22).

Weighing the matter carefully, I did not dare to be found wanting. Leaving the denomination had been a big test in obedience. Now could it be that giving up the "cushion" of savings was test number two? David was the head of our home, and I felt more peace in complying with his wishes than in refusing.

"All right," I rather reluctantly agreed. "You can write out the check."

It would be lovely to report that we lived happily ever after, that money just rolled in and we never had a concern. But we all know where liars go (see Revelation 21:8), so one must be truthful.

If I didn't fail the test on lying, I did on being fearful and unbelieving. I worried. I really worried. We were both fifty-nine years old. Every time a friend or acquaintance lost his job for one reason or another, I would lose a little more sleep. Even slight recessions are felt immediately by ministries existing on gifts. We had already forfeited our denominational pension. If David were jobless. . . . We weren't yet eligible for Social Security. Ann was a junior at Oral Roberts University. . . .

I reviewed our situation continually.

That was over ten years ago. The Lord has been faithful. In fact, so many major needs have been so quietly met I almost feel as though we took out a policy on the Divine Insurance Program. And I like to think that, when we get to heaven, some perfect strangers will be waiting to tell us, "It was through your gift that we came to Jesus."

21–"Go to the spa"

Would that everybody could have an Aunt Verona! She seems ageless. In her nineties, she still maintains and runs the Ziegler Motel in New Bern, North Carolina. Always the horticulturist, she has azaleas growing almost as high as her motel units--a perfect delight each April.

Aunt Verona was married to Mother's brother, Jacob Ziegler, and gave him tender loving care when he suffered untold pain from an accident and unsuccessful surgeries. For sixteen years she stayed by him, nursing him and running the motel at the same time. Nurses would come and go, worn out, but plucky Aunt Verona stayed on. Upon his death in 1967, she refused to let anyone say it had been a burden.

"It's never a burden when you love someone," she would answer.

Once she was showing me a scrapbook she had made for him to enjoy. Several women in the pictures weren't familiar to me.

"Oh, they were some of Jacob's former girl friends. They were so lovely," she'd explain in her North Carolina drawl.

Aunt Verona has a picture of Jesus in every motel room and the sign of the fish on her highway sign. And Aunt Verona hears from God and does what He tells her to do.

Once our Barbara was planning a trip home from Israel. One could hardly call Barbara's visits vacations. Moved to come home by Gwen's having a baby, or Ann's getting married, or somebody's moving, or my not being too well, Barbara usually works hard every day she is here. This particular visit had been very strenuous, and she was about to return in three days.

In the middle of the day, Aunt Verona called. That was unusual. Generally she calls after 10 P.M., when guests are bedded down for the night.

"Peggy, I have the oddest feeling Barbara needs money, and I am to send her a check."

Now I have always hated it when God's servants seem to have their hands out for gifts continually. So I try to steer clear of being like that.

"Oh no, Aunt Verona! Thank you, but I'm sure she's all right. Her return ticket is purchased. Thank you just the same." We visited for quite some time. Since Aunt Verona's not much for letter writing, she uses the phone instead. Barbara, in a nearby room, heard the entire conversation but said nothing.

Just as we were finishing, Aunt Verona said, "I can't shake the idea I'm to send Barbara money. Tell her I'm putting a check for $500 in the mail right away, so she'll have it before she leaves." I thanked her again and hung up.

"All right, Barbara," I called. "'Fess up now. What do you need money for?"

Since she never tells anybody but the Lord her needs, I really couldn't imagine the problem.

"Well," she said, "the day I get back I must pay three months' rent in advance. I reminded the Lord this morning that I didn't have it!" Needless to say, Aunt Verona's $500 came in very handy.

One Friday evening in 1983, dinner was about to be served in the Omni Hotel in Norfolk. Five-hundred people had gathered from fifty states for a Partners Seminar--a meeting held quarterly for some of people who supported CBN. They were chosen by computer, so each area had equal representation.

David was in charge of counseling. I sat at a table on the mezzanine and acted as secretary. Folks wanting an appointment signed up for one of several counselors on duty at free hours.

All teams had been paired off and gone to conference rooms. David had just returned from his final appointment when a man, obviously not very happy, came up and said he would like to talk with somebody. David immediately took him down the hall. When he returned--late for dinner--he was smiling.

Later, as we went to our room, David reported. "That man is a writer. He often has articles in national magazines. He was quite upset.

"'I need to talk to somebody,' he began. 'I'm here only because my wife goes for this sort of thing. I am opposed to everything you people stand for. I am a member of the ACLU, on the board of *Mother Jones* magazine [a Socialist publication], etc., etc.'"

As David prayed for wisdom, he thought over his options. Having graduated from Antioch College, he knew the liberal viewpoint only too well. But why get involved in that? Instead, he decided to present Jesus, telling the man in simple terms why He had to come to earth and what His death meant for sinners. Before long, they were praying the sinner's prayer. Then they prayed for the man to be baptized in the Holy Spirit. He received the whole package.

When we left the closing brunch on Sunday, we saw the man and his wife at the Robertsons' table, laughing and enjoying a great exchange.

Two years later, close to the time of David's retirement, the man and his wife returned for a visit to CBN. He looked David up and reported, "I've gotten out of the ACLU, resigned from the *Mother Jones* board, and turned my life around since I met the Lord."

Thanks be to God, who always gives us the victory, I thought.

The Lord granted David favor during his six years at CBN. The last Christmas he was there, he was one of several-dozen employees given the President's Award for Excellence. His was the last name to be called, and a friend told me he was given a standing ovation by all the employees--some five or six hundred--who were present at that time.

Five farewell parties made our departure from CBN a pleasant memory. The last week David was there, Pat Robertson interviewed him on "The 700 Club" nationwide. David was able to tell of his plans to give full attention to intercession for a Holy Ghost, heaven-sent, repentance-producing revival. Meanwhile, the Lord kept on teaching me obedience.

"Go to the spa!"

No, Lord, that can't be You, I thought. Rain was pounding on the den window. It was the ideal day to begin packing. David and I were ready for retirement and hoped this would be our last move. After many moves in our forty-three years of marriage, the job didn't get any easier, but one did know how to go about it.

"Go to the spa!" The instruction wasn't audible, exactly, but I had come to recognize the proddings of the Holy Spirit. Nevertheless, logic again prevailed, and I kept up my argument.

"Lord, You see the rain. It's a dreadful day outdoors. Besides, I haven't had any good witnessing opportunities at the spa lately," I continued lamely, as I dusted off the fourth volume of the *Encyclopedia Britannica* and stored it in the carton.

"Go to the spa!" Now it was firm. Frankly, I was afraid not to go.

"All right," I answered, like a rebellious child forced into obedience. Grabbing my raincoat and gathering up my spa bag, purse, and keys, I headed out the door.

Once at the pool, I surveyed my prospects. A woman was in the center of the pool, and a few others were at the edge. Not wanting to waste time, I went right to the woman in the middle and got into a conver-

sation. Within a few sentences, I followed my usual procedure of dropping the words "700 Club." If there was
any spiritual interest or thirst, it helped people to know
where I was coming from.

This woman, though polite, didn't bite at my bait. "I
must be off," she said shortly. "I've got an appointment."

After swimming briefly, I decided to head home
and get back to my packing. Mounting the pool steps, I
was about to murmur and complain to the Lord about a
useless trip, when a timid little woman standing there
spoke up.

"Did you say you're from 'The 700 Club'?" she
asked.

"Yes," I said, pausing on the steps.

"I need to talk to you."

Returning to the water, I suggested we cross the
pool, so we could have privacy. As we held onto the
side, we flutter-kicked, conveying the idea we were exer-
cising.

"I'm having a terrible problem with my marriage,"
she said tearfully. "It's all but over." Now I knew why the
Lord had sent me there.

"Have you ever given your heart to Jesus?" I asked.

"Not really. I never quite knew how," she replied.

"It's really very simple," I explained. "The Bible tells
us we all have sinned, but 'if we confess our sins, he is
faithful and just to forgive us our sins, and to cleanse us
from all unrighteousness' [1 John 1:9]. If you would like,
you can pray this prayer after me--and if you mean it in
your heart, Jesus will forgive your sins and make you
His child."

Readily she followed as I led in a simple petition:
"Dear Lord, please forgive me my sins; come into my
heart, and make me Your child. In Jesus' name. Amen."
Then we asked the Holy Spirit to guide us as we dis-

cussed her problem. The Lord seemed to outline a procedure for her to follow:

First, she would purchase a helpful book on marriage--my favorite, *You Can Be the Wife of a Happy Husband.* Then she would try to find good fellowship for Bible-study and prayer. Her husband, as head of the home, was to be loved and honored. We prayed for the Lord's balance in every aspect of her life: appearance, finances, children, homemaking, in-laws, and spiritual pursuits.

She would try to put her husband's needs first and keep her own interests in proper perspective. As we closed with prayer, she seemed eager to return home. She felt confident she saw her role in a new light. We climbed back up the steps.

I couldn't resist saying, "The Lord must surely love you. I hadn't planned to come today, but He drew me. He knew we needed to talk."

With tears rolling down her cheeks, she confided, "This morning I was so low, I felt I couldn't go on. I lay on the bedroom floor and told God He had to send me help, and it had to be *today.*"

As I drove home, the rain had a soothing effect. My heart was light. To think Almighty God had an assignment and had chosen me to fill it! It was exhilarating, and I told Him so.

"Anytime, Lord. I'm always available--anytime at all."

22--"Go for it!"

In June of 1985, Barbara came from Israel and helped us move from our Virginia Beach townhouse.

"This will be our hardest assignment yet," David warned as we headed north. The Lord's instructions were to settle in Lititz, Pennsylvania, and pray for our church and denomination to be revived.

Our housing provision had been yet another miracle. Sitting in the mission house in Bluefields, Nicaragua, one day back in 1956, David had asked, "Where would you most like to retire?"

"Oh, I could be happy most any place," I answered, thinking back over the five states where we had lived. "But there is just one house I would really enjoy. That's the little old Huebener house in Lititz. It will doubtless be left to the church--but even if the church would sell it, there is no way we could buy it." I never gave it another thought.

The Huebeners were not relatives of ours, just very dear friends. Miss Mary Huebener was Mother's best friend and always spent holidays and special occasions in our home. I called her "Aunt Mary." She and her brother lived in the charming family home, built in 1762 in the heart of town. Both the brothers had married, but neither had children.

After we had resettled in the States and were living in Ephraim, Wisconsin, the phone rang one afternoon. It was my brother Richard, the lawyer.

"Aunt Mary died today," he announced, "and you'll be happy to learn she has left you the house and everything in it." (There was a clause that books and papers of historical interest should go to the church archives.)

The Lord had done it again! Far beyond our fondest hopes, He handed us the house of our dreams for retirement.

Returning to my hometown was pure joy for both of us--and Mother was happy about it too. She and my stepfather came up from West Virginia for a visit in September, and we had an early celebration of her one-hundredth birthday, due December 8.

On the evening of September 10, as we prepared for bed, David gave an announcement I knew was of the Lord: "Beginning tomorrow, the Lord wants me to get up about four o'clock and go out to the cemetery and pray for revival."

That was more than five years ago. Except for rare occasions--usually because of being out of town--he hasn't missed a day. At first, the policemen on their rounds checked him out, but now they know his mission.

One experience bears telling. On the morning of March 26, 1987, near four o'clock, David was walking south on Cedar Street, toward the cemetery. He had been discouraged at the lack of results and was asking the Lord if he had heard Him aright. Suddenly he felt a presence. Thinking someone was right behind him, he felt the hair stand up on his neck.

Then the sweetest, most melodious voice he had ever heard said, *"Go for it!"* That was all.

The fear left, and David looked around. Nobody was there. It was the first time the Lord had ever spoken to him in an audible voice. Twenty-one years earlier, on the same date, God's instructions to leave the denomination had been given through Ezekiel 12:3, which ends, "It may be they will consider, though they be a rebellious house." Now the Lord was encouraging David to continue his prayers that "they will consider."

Oh, how I yearned for them to "consider."

On the first Sunday after our return to Lititz, I was sitting in the Sunday-school auditorium, and my sixty-five-year-old mind went back well over fifty years. I saw myself marching into Vacation Bible School singing, "Onward, Christian soldiers, marching as to war. . . . " How I had wanted to march in that battle! Now the Lord had shown me the whole picture, and my desire to march to His tune was stronger than ever.

Later, sitting in church, I was reminded of a morning service back in the thirties, when I was in my teens. During closing prayer, my heart had been "strangely warmed," and I had told the Lord I wanted to serve Him in this church when I grew up. As we raised our heads, tears were in my eyes. I kept talking to the Lord in my heart: "Lord, I feel so sorry for You. Out of all these people, nobody loves You more than I. And nobody has less to give." I knew I had nothing to commend me: no scholastic achievement or leadership ability. But I loved the Lord and wanted to be a blessing to Him.

Another memory was of sitting on a bench at the cemetery. I had many theological questions, and I didn't know where to get the answers. "Lord," I had said silently, "there should be a place, in the center of town, where one could go and talk over problems and have prayer."

Now, half a century later, David and I were being stationed in the center of town for just such a purpose. In many ways, this is an odd assignment. Outwardly, we can do nothing. Privately, we are engaged in spiritual warfare, "not against flesh and blood, but against principalities, against powers, against the rulers of the darkness of this world, against spiritual wickedness in high places," and our weapon is "the sword of the Spirit, which is the word of God" (Ephesians 6:12,17).

There is much that we don't know, but we do know that the stakes are high.

"There's one thing I want to know more than anything else. When I see Jesus, I'm going to ask Him," I said, stirring my coffee as the Sunday-school class was gathering one morning.

"What's that?" Nancy asked.

"How many folks are really saved and on their way to heaven." Here I paused. I wanted to say, "in our church," but felt that might be offensive. Instead I finished the sentence with "in our town."

"What difference would it make?" Don asked.

"A big one," I answered. "If it's as few as I fear, our job is enormous. But if almost all are ready, we can relax."

That ended the discussion, which reflected our mounting concern. David and I have a tremendous burden for the lost. If we ourselves could once have been so active in the Lord's work and still have been lost, it stands to reason that many others who feel "safe" are not really born again and on their way to heaven.

Common opinion seems to be that, if there is a heaven and one leads a good life--injures no man, gives to the poor, belongs to church--he has it made. The people of Noah's day mocked him as he prepared the ark of safety. People today mock preachers of righteousness, too. Calling believers "fanatics," they congratulate themselves they are making it without causing any ripples in the pond.

Ever since our conversion some thirty years before, as we studied Scripture, David and I had become more and more alarmed. Seminaries of mainline churches have, by and large, conveniently omitted all references to or warnings about hell. Conversely, the assurance of heaven has been weakened. The usual answer to the question, "Do you believe you'll go to heaven?" is "I hope so," or "I'm trying." The fact that we get there only by trusting in the atoning blood of Jesus is rarely mentioned.

Once the authority of the Bible is put in question, there are no absolutes. You make your own rules. Hence, some people might answer the question regarding an assurance of heaven with no doubt in their minds. As one speaker put it, the unbeliever makes his own God and so, naturally, has a good relationship with Him; but in the believer's case, God is making the person. . . .

Class started, and my remark was forgotten. An hour later, I was sitting in church. The offering was being taken. My mind was in neutral.

"Eighty-four," came to me clearly.

"How odd," I said to myself. "Eighty-four. That doesn't make sense."

"Eighty-four." There it came again.

That number means nothing, I thought.

"Eighty-four," a third time. (This all happened in seconds.)

"Oh, dear Lord! You are telling me that only eighty-four people are saved--one in fifteen of our congregation. How alarming!"

As I looked out over the congregation, living comfortably and assuming all was well, I knew why Jesus wept over Jerusalem and said,

"O Jerusalem, Jerusalem, thou that killest the prophets, and stonest them which are sent unto thee, how often would I have gathered thy children together, even as a hen gathereth her chickens under her wings, and ye would not!"

(Matthew 23:37)

I had returned from a spiritual journey of forty years eager to share my discovery of Jesus and the Holy Spirit with my friends. But very few wanted to hear.

I have often felt like the little boy in the story, "The Emperor's New Clothes." All were told only the intelligent could see the emperor's new royal attire. As people *oohed* and *aahed* and pretended they saw beautiful finery, the youngster put it plainly: "He's in his *underwear!*"

The prevailing theology of mainline denominational churches (those in the National Council of Churches) calls for the mind to struggle with their latest theories.

My theology would be more like that of the blind man healed by Jesus: *"One thing I know, that, whereas I was blind, now I see"* (John 9:25).

When one is born again by trusting Christ as his personal Savior, he faces a dilemma. Should he selfishly keep quiet, clutching to himself the marvelous revelation that he now has his valid passport to heaven and is assured everlasting joy and bliss? In this way, he offends nobody.

Or should he seek to warn others, who may be unaware of the hell awaiting them? The good news is: you *can* know Jesus, one on one, and receive pardon for sin. The bad news is: you *must*.

When I innocently started my search as a schoolgirl, I little dreamed I would end up in such a quandary. When folks slip away to the next life, I feel convicted if I did nothing to make sure they were aware of their options. There's an old hymn that expresses our concern:

I dreamed I searched heaven for you,
Searched vainly through heaven for you.
Friend, won't you prepare to meet me up there,
Lest we should search heaven for you?

Roy, a friend of ours, tells of hearing two pastors on the radio. They were discussing what percentage of church members are really saved. The first estimated between eight and twelve percent. The second one felt that was too high. His guess was in the five-to-seven-percent bracket.

Suppose the radio ministers were right, and ten percent or fewer in the average church are truly born again. Translated, that means nine out of ten are going to a dreadful hell. Would that these things weren't so! But the Bible says the way is narrow, "and few there be that find it" (Matthew 7:14).

The *Lancaster New Era* for April 12, 1991, reported on a survey released by "an ICR Survey Research Group of Media," tabulating the answers to questions posed over a thirteen-month period to a sample of 113,000 adults. According to the survey, seven out of eight Americans say they identify with a Christian denomination. I wish the questions had included those used by Dr. D. James Kennedy in "Evangelism Explosion," a program for soul-winning:

1. Have you come to the place in your spiritual life where you know for certain if you were to die today you would go to heaven?
2. Suppose you were to die today and stand before God and He were to say to you, "Why should I let you into my heaven?" What would you say?

I wonder what percentage of the seven out of eight adults who "identify with a Christian denomination" could give assurance--and the basis for it--that they are truly saved.

In our congregation in Ephraim, a prosperous businessman attended services each summer. You didn't talk to him long before you realized he had one consuming worry: the fact that Jesus said,

> *"It is easier for a camel to go through the eye of a needle, than for a rich man to enter into the kingdom of God."* (Matthew 19:24)

Thank goodness the man reverenced the Word of God! I trust he met Jesus face to face and is in heaven by now.

A man in another of our congregations was very sick. Either he died for a few seconds or he had a dream. He was being hurled through space. Over to his left was a large black hole. He knew it led to hell. He was being sucked toward it and was helpless to stop himself. Just as he got to it, he floated away and returned to his body. From that time on, he took a bold stand for the Lord, even preaching on the post-office steps. His "Amens" from the pew were tolerated by a sympathetic congregation in our traditional, quiet church.

When did you last hear from your pulpit the sins that keep you from heaven? Yet the New Testament contains several lists of sinners that will be excluded. You can read them for yourself:

> *Being filled with all unrighteousness, fornication, wickedness, covetousness, maliciousness; full of envy, murder, debate, deceit, malignity, whisperers, backbiters, haters of God, despiteful, proud, boasters, inventors of evil things, disobedient to parents, without understanding, without natural affection, implacable, unmerciful: who knowing the judgment of God, that they which commit such things are worthy of death, not only do the same, but have pleasure in them that do them. . . .* (Romans 1:29-32)

> *Know ye not that the unrighteous shall not inherit the kingdom of God? Be not deceived: neither fornicators, nor idolators, nor adulterers, nor effeminate, nor abusers of themselves with mankind, nor thieves, nor covetous, nor drunkards, nor revilers, nor extortioners shall inherit the kingdom of God.* (I Corinthians 6:9,10)

> *Now the works of the flesh are manifest, which are these: Adultery, fornication, uncleanness, lasciviousness, idolatry, witchcraft, hatred, variance, emulations, wrath, strife, seditions, heresies, envy-*

ings, murders, drunkenness, revellings, and such like: of the which I tell you before, as I have also told you in time past, that they which do such things shall not inherit the kingdom of God.

(Galatians 5:19-21)

But the fearful, and unbelieving, and the abominable, and murderers, and whoremongers, and sorcerers, and idolaters, and all liars shall have their part in the lake which burneth with fire and brimstone: which is the second death.

(Revelation 21:8)

The lists are awesome. Read them again. If you practice any of those sins, without repentance, you cannot inherit the kingdom of God. Period. Those of us never tempted by sexual sins tend to feel smug until we come across covetousness, for instance--or idolatry, both of which take a multitude to hell. I know, because idolatry almost took me. For years, my church was my god. But neither the loveliness of the sanctuary, the moving traditions, or the music, composed to glorify God, can be allowed to take the place of God or receive the glory due only to Him and His Son, Jesus. Nothing in this world is worth going to hell for all eternity. Nothing, *nothing*, **nothing**.

Who can claim exemption from every sin? Not one. The Bible says *all* have sinned. Here is where the great and glorious gift of atonement enters in.

While living in Virginia Beach, we attended a Monday-evening prayer-and-praise service at the home of Bob and Gloria Barnaby. A young Navy wife led us in praise, and with the help of her guitar gave us the chorus I can never forget. It says it all.

I am covered over with the precious blood of Jesus,
And He lives in me, He lives in me.

I am covered over with the robe of righteousness
    He gives to me, He gives to me.
What a joy it is to know,
    my heavenly Father loves me so,
    And gives to me--my Jesus.
And when He looks at me,
    He sees not what I used to be,
    But He sees Jesus.

How beautiful! Are you covered with that robe? If not, you can be by simply inviting Jesus into your heart.

When we express to loved ones our concern about their salvation, we are frequently met with the accusation, "You're being judgmental." If, perchance, the individual to whom we speak is already saved, he (or she) is usually grateful someone cared enough to check. So perhaps the degree of irritation is a measure of the need.

Our son-in-law, Rick Hanger, tells of a freak tide that occurred when he was a boy living in Virginia Beach. One morning, as he went out early to get the newspaper, he could scarcely believe his eyes. The Atlantic Ocean was rolling in over the dunes, and it was obvious that lovely beach homes were going to be inundated. After alerting his mother, he rushed across the street to the home of a retiree neighbor with an invalid wife.

He rang the bell and waited. Eventually the man appeared in his pajamas and robe, angry at being disturbed.

"What do you want at this hour?" he bellowed.

"Sir, the ocean is in your yard and will soon be at your door!"

The man hadn't a moment to lose in getting his wife and himself dressed, into the car, and off to higher ground. I'm sure his original anger turned to gratitude.

No, we're not judging. We are warning. The Bible judges. Jesus said it clearly in just five words: "Ye *must* be born again: (John 3:7; italics added). Church membership, change-the-world marches, generous giving, and good works don't provide a ticket to heaven.

There is only one door, and that is the Lord Jesus Christ. He came and laid down His life for our sins. When we humbly come to Him, acknowledging our sinfulness, asking forgiveness, and inviting Him into our hearts, then and only then are our names written in the Lamb's Book of Life, assuring us of one of those mansions Jesus said He was going to prepare for us.

The choice is ours. But in order to receive forgiveness for sin, we must humble ourselves and become like little children.

The night David and I knelt by our couch in the Riverside parsonage, we knew nothing except that we were lacking. And all we said was, "Lord, show us what is missing." He showed us Jesus, whom to know is life eternal. "Him that cometh to me I will in no wise cast out" (John 6:37). What a promise!

Exciting days are ahead. Next to come is the latter rain, which means revival. Parts of Africa are already seeing it, as are some countries in Central and South America. After this, we expect Jesus to appear in the clouds and call His saved ones up in the Rapture. There in heaven, while the world goes through great tribulation--the worst ever--we will enjoy the marriage feast of the Lamb. We feel conditions are such we may well see this before the century ends. Until that glorious day, we've been given a challenge:

Stand up, stand up for Jesus,
The strife will not be long;
This day the noise of battle,
The next the victor's song:
To him that overcometh
A crown of life shall be;
He with the King of Glory
Shall reign eternally.

George Duffield

There seem to be many sincere church people for whom our testimony raises a question regarding their salvation. If you are not certain about your salvation, I recommend that you seek the Lord for assurance. You might pray something like this:

Lord, if I have not really entered in and my name has not been written in the Lamb's Book of Life, I want it there. Please lead me until that is accomplished.

On the other hand, if you *know* you have never meaningfully prayed to accept Jesus as your Savior, maybe you'd like to take this opportunity to invite Him into your heart. Here is a prayer you might use:

Father, I know "all have sinned, and come short of the glory of God" [Romans 3:23]. I know too that "the wages of sin is death; but the gift of God is eternal life through Jesus Christ our Lord" [Romans 6:23]. I now repent of my sins and ask Your forgiveness.

I confess with my mouth the Lord Jesus and believe in my heart You raised Him from the dead [see Romans 10:9]. By Your power and grace, I claim that salvation is mine. Thank you, Jesus, for saving

Peggy Jones

me. Holy Spirit, come dwell within my soul and mind and be my Teacher. In Jesus' name. Amen.

Now that you *know* your name is written in the Lamb's Book of Life, how about helping us to seek and to save other lost sheep and rescue them for everlasting life in heaven? Join us in continuing to pray for that Holy Ghost, heaven-sent, repentance-producing revival that is so desperately needed in our sin-sick world.

The Lord has commanded us to pray, and He has promised that He will hear from heaven. We couldn't ask for more.

THE END

For a free catalog of other inspiring books
lifting up the Light of the world
send self-addressed stamped (2 stamps) envelope to:
Star Books, inc.
408 Pearson Street
Wilson, NC 27893